LETTERS HOME FROM WORLD WAR II

St. Louis

MESSAGES OF HOPE AND HEARTBREAK FROM THE FRONT LINES

Christopher Alan Gordon

REEDY PRESS

Reedy Press
PO Box 5131
St. Louis, MO 63139
reedypress.com

Library of Congress Control Number: 2025943631
ISBN: 9781681066042

Design by Jill Halpin

Unless otherwise indicated, all photos are courtesy of the author or in the public domain.

Cover image courtesy of National Archives.

Printed in the United States of America
25 26 27 28 29   5 4 3 2 1

This book is dedicated to the men and women of the St. Louis region who fought and died for the cause of freedom and democracy in World War II. May their sacrifices never be forgotten.

CONTENTS

INTRODUCTION

Letters Home from World War II: St. Louis tells the story of World War II as experienced by the men and women of the St. Louis region who served, fought, and died in a war that tested the will of so many and ultimately transformed the world. The letters included in this volume present an eyewitness account of one of history's greatest global conflicts, and they tell the story like no other. Reading the words, written as the authors were enduring the loneliness, anxiety, and uncertainty of war far from home, is the best way to genuinely understand the times and events of the war years.

The letter writers came from all walks of life: urban neighborhoods, rural communities, white, black, Asian, working class, middle class, and wealthy families. Each person put aside their life, family, and career to fight for their country and stand up to powerful forces that practiced and promoted terror, hatred, and authoritarianism. Through newspaper accounts, military records, and other sources, I've attempted to reconstruct the experiences of these soldiers, sailors, auxiliary members, and civilians. Unfortunately, much has been lost to the passage of time, including many service records that burned in the tragic fire that consumed volumes of documents held in the National Archives and Records Administration's National Personnel Records Center in St. Louis in 1973. However, the letters themselves help bring these men and women to life.

Author's note:

The letters printed in this book are transcribed as written by their authors to better reflect the characteristics of the soldiers, sailors, and other individuals who wrote them. Only a few minor corrections have been made to allow them to be more easily read. In some instances, information that I deemed to be irrelevant, such as postal addresses, or comments that might violate the privacy of the individual or their families, were omitted.

ACKNOWLEDGMENTS

This book relies on primary sources from archives and repositories across the St. Louis region. Without the assistance of the helpful staff at each one, I would not have found the information I needed, and my research would have been twice as difficult. A tremendous amount of gratitude is due to all the dedicated archivists everywhere for the assistance they provided me and the work they do every day to assist researchers of all ages.

I want to particularly thank archivist A. J. Medlock and his staff at The State Historical Society of Missouri; Michele Levandoski, director, School Sisters of Notre Dame North American Archives; Kelly Plunkett, museum curator, Jefferson Barracks Park, St. Louis County Parks and Recreation; Amy Haake, archivist and chief administrative officer, St. Charles County Historical Society; Lauren Jarvis and Dennis Northcott, archivists, Missouri Historical Society Archives; Randy Blomquist, assistant librarian, Missouri Historical Society Library; Lauren Sallwasser, associate photo archivist, Missouri Historical Society; and the staff of the St. Louis Public Library Manuscripts Collection and the invaluable staff of the National Archives National Personnel Records Center in Spanish Lake, Missouri.

A special thanks goes to Judy Kaufman for allowing me to include the Risch family letters. As her family's archivist, Judy has done a fantastic job of documenting her uncle's military service.

It is a privilege to work with all of you.

Soldier writing letter. *National Archives*

MORALE IS A LOT OF LITTLE THINGS

Most Americans would have preferred to stay out of the war. Yet, there was little chance that America could remain neutral. This conflict was not an isolated dispute between two countries, it was an all-out conflict encompassing the whole of Europe and half of Asia. Then Pearl Habor changed everything. The staggering loss of life suffered on December 7, 1941, brought the sobering realities of war to a nation that had enjoyed relative peace since the end of World War I in 1918. Americans understood that they could not stand to the side any longer. The enemies were at the gates and American blood had been shed.

Japan's surprise attack unnerved all Americans, and a sudden sense of insecurity, fear, and anger seized the American people. No foreign nation had attacked American soil since the war of 1812 nearly 130 years prior. Fear produced rumors of saboteurs and a possible coastal invasion, which kept people all over the country on edge. Then, four days after Pearl Harbor, Germany declared war on the US, adding to the unease. Germany and Italy always had been the main concern of President Franklin D. Roosevelt and many other Americans. Now that concern had come to pass, and Americans faced the reality of fighting a war on two continents and across two oceans. Roosevelt spoke of it as the Second World War.

A series of dramatic and demoralizing events compounded America's newfound vulnerability. The daily newspapers seemed to bring nothing but bad news in the days, weeks, and months following Pearl Harbor. The first was the unsettling number of American and British merchant ships torpedoed and sunk by German U-boats (some within miles of America's Atlantic Coast), many of them taking the lives of those onboard. Then came the heart-wrenching news that the Japanese had forced the surrender of thousands of American soldiers in the Philippines and sent them off to prisoner of war camps. Nothing could prepare the American public for such a blow.

Then, in April 1941, finally came some news that provided a bit of a morale boost for those Americans eager to hit back at Japan. US Army Air Force General Jimmy Doolittle had launched a surprise attack on the Japanese mainland. Flying B-24 Mitchell bombers off the deck of the USS *Hornet*, he bombed industrial targets in Tokyo. It was a big gamble, but it paid off. It proved that America could reach the island of Japan and bring the war to them while also providing Americans with some degree of satisfaction that Pearl Harbor could be avenged.

However, the news remained mostly dismal. In the first two years of the war, Germany and Japan continued to push forward, win decisive battles, and occupy new countries. The Axis powers seemed not only fearfully strong but also entrenched and unstoppable, a concept that withered American morale. However, President Roosevelt and top officials in Washington knew that we were still unprepared for an all-out war. With this understanding,

Roosevelt and his commanders decided that the priority for 1942 would not be launching counterattacks and raids but training men, building ships and planes, and manufacturing guns, shells, bombs, and other military hardware.

Total war meant changes in the lifestyles of most Americans. Still, the only way to win the war was for Americans to go all in and contribute however they could. On the home front, Americans had to come to terms with rationing, travel restrictions, and civil defense drills. Everyone had to do their part. Roosevelt and the War Department understood that unity was the key to Allied victory. Americans must stick together, sacrifice, and stay focused on producing the essential supplies, equipment, and resources that our soldiers and sailors had to have to get the job done. Only then would things begin to change for the better. Only then could our enemies be defeated.

Everyone agreed that raising public morale and confidence was important, but troop morale was the top priority for military commanders. A focused, driven, and purposeful fighting force was an effective and determined fighting force. Keeping soldiers and sailors healthy and happy was as important as their combat training. Now, for the first time, America's defensive capabilities employed something besides all the most advanced battleships, aircraft, weapons, and bombs. This modern military arsenal included the power of motion pictures, radio, and live entertainment. The War Department assigned the task of keeping up the morale of servicemen to two branches of the US Army: the Signal Corps and Armed Forces Radio.

Beginning in 1942, the Armed Forces Radio Network started broadcasting via shortwave radio. Servicemen and women around the globe tuned in to hear the swinging rhythms of Glenn Miller, Duke Ellington, and Benny Goodman. Comedians like Jack Benny and ventriloquist Edgar Bergen voicing the sarcastic quips of his dummy partner, Charlie McCarthy, kept soldiers, sailors, and nurses in stitches. Gathering around the radio in some barracks far away or on a ship at sea reminded those listening that although it wasn't the same, it was as close as you could get to being back home in your living room surrounded by the ones you loved.

Keeping things upbeat was also an important element of the messaging. The Army used a variety of techniques to keep up the soldiers' confidence and brighten their day such as incorporating "Messages of Cheer to Army Personnel" to broadcast across the radio network to hospitalized, wounded, or seriously ill soldiers. By filling out form W.D., A.G.O. No. 222, a personal radiogram message could be sent to a certain someone in recovery. The Army's set parameters for the message were that it had to be sent by the soldier's designated emergency contact person, it could be no longer than five words, and it had to be cheerful.

While radio supplied the familiar sounds of live entertainment, film provided the visuals that brought the sights of home to the battlefront. The Signal Corps employed nearly 30,000 personnel to maintain film libraries and an intricate system of film distribution centers worldwide. This elaborate distribution system gave our troops access to Hollywood's latest movies and hundreds of educational and training films. For a generation of young Americans who had grown up attending afternoon matinees at neighborhood and small-town movie theaters, few things could ease the tensions and horrors of war like indulging in the familiar world of Tinseltown productions. As one War Department documentary, *Movies at War*, noted at the time, "Hollywood features provide a brief respite from the teeth-chattering thunder of battle." They transported the men and women serving on the front lines to a happier place far from the enemy.

But for all the military's efforts to bring a slice of America to those far from home and despite everything Hollywood could produce, nothing boosted the morale of America's fighting men and women like a letter from their loved ones back home. It was the one thing that all the generals, admirals, and sergeants in the military could not provide—a little piece of home you could hold in your hand.

The precious lines scribbled across the paper hearkened the voices of mothers, fathers, sisters and brothers, wives or sweethearts, clergymen and neighbors, and old school buddies. These small packets of hope reminded fighting men that one day the horrors of the war would be behind them, peace would be restored, and they would return to the loved ones they left behind. This is what they were fighting for.

Getting letters from home was the difference between a good day and a bad day for soldiers and sailors. As Private John E. Washington wrote in his war diary, "Sure feels bad when mail call comes and I haven't any." Getting a letter kept that emotional bond alive across the thousands of miles of separation. It brought smiles to faces in a time when the grim reality of survival was the typical focus of your day. The *Washington Citizen* in Franklin County, Missouri, printed a quote from one US Marine in 1943 on the subject of letters: "You go through your battles and you don't want to think about them. You want to relax some way. Then you hear the mail is coming. When the sacks come, it doesn't seem as if you could wait while they sort the envelopes out."

The military took great pains to implore loved ones who were writing to their soldiers and sailors not to send news that might distract or depress the receiver. "Keep it cheerful" was the mantra. As one Army lieutenant told a group of Henry County, Missouri, Kiwanis Club members in 1944, "Most of the boys are more concerned about the welfare of their folks at home than they are with their own comfort and safety. Always write cheerful letters," he said, "if you can't write cheerful letters, don't write at all." He emphasized his point by telling those gathered of a soldier who received bad news from home while he was already suffering under mental strain. The soldier, noted the lieutenant, "cracked up" when he received the "blue, sad letter."

Receiving a letter meant taking time to answer that letter, and most servicemen were good about doing so. According to the *Washington Citizen* article, a survey of American servicemen in England found that 43 percent of off-duty personnel spent their nights off writing at least one letter home, 36 percent wrote two, 14 percent wrote three, and seven percent "scratched away at four or more." However the letters from servicemen were not always received in the exact form as they were written. The US military implemented a strict censorship system to prevent sensitive information from falling into enemy hands. Censors would read through letters, blacking out any mention of troop locations, planned movements, or military operations. Servicemen understood the necessity of this censorship, but it often made communication difficult. Families at home sometimes received letters filled with blank spaces with the words cut away with an X-Acto knife, leaving them to wonder about their loved one's safety and whereabouts.

Unlike letters from the Civil War or World War I, in which soldiers wrote openly about their whereabouts and what they had seen and experienced, the servicemen and women of World War II had to write in generalities. Using phrases such "somewhere in France" or "somewhere in the Pacific," soldiers and sailors did their best to let loved ones know where they were.

Horrific details were also kept out of correspondence. The death of a comrade might be mentioned but only briefly. Anything deemed sensitive was scrutinized by censors. If a letter from a loved one or soldier writing back home was determined to be filled with too much classified information or even news from the home front that might be deemed demoralizing, the letter could be returned to the sender with a note asking them to rewrite it. Censorship proved to be a slow and complicated process.

One Navy commander, Frederick J. Nelson, criticized the military's censorship procedures and rules as too encumbering for the fast delivery of the mail. Everyone agreed that censorship was necessary, he argued, but not when it slowed the delivery of mail to men who were hunger for news from back home or eager to answer letters. Slow delivery times were bad for morale. Nelson lamented that some officers were discouraging their men from writing too

Francis Weidler served as an Army censor in Britain and France. He sent home this "censored" Christmas card for Christmas 1943. *Collections of the Missouri Historical Society*

often or encouraging them to limit the number of pages so that it would not burden the mail system. This was detrimental, he argued: "A fighter must have an outlet for his sentiments. He needs some vehicle to get his thoughts to those he knows will value his opinions and who have a sympathetic understanding of his type of human nature." The system needed streamlining according to his thought, and the military was slow to address it.

The Army and Navy were tasked with enforcing all personnel and press censorship. It was an arduous job, given the thousands of letters streaming back home from soldiers and sailors. Navy censors read an average of 30 letters a day, each averaging about 2,000 words. This was about 60,000 words per day. Of those 60,000, however, one source noted that only about 10 words per day were censored. This is a realistic assessment since a significant number of service members' letters mention that they cannot say much about the specifics of their location or duties because the letters will be censored. They generally followed the rules.

Sometimes a unit's commanding officer had the chore of reading and censoring the letters of their men. For one bomber group commander, this was one of the more entertaining aspects of his job. When Robert Fischer responded to his girlfriend's inquiry about his involvement in censorship work, he replied humorously, "You are quite right about censoring being an interesting job. After a while to save time, you just read certain guy's mail, especially those addressed to 'Miss' or 'Mrs.,' if it is someone else's wife."

As the volume of wartime mail increased, so did the need for an efficient postal system. The military faced a significant challenge

The 6888th or "Six Triple Eight" Postal Battalion had the gargantuan chore of sorting the backlog of soldiers' mail accumulating in warehouses in England and France. *National Archives*

in ensuring letters reached the correct recipients, particularly in the chaos of war. This was where the 6888th Central Postal Directory Battalion, known as the "Six Triple Eight," played a crucial role. This all-black, all-female unit, led by US Army Major Charity Adams, was assigned the daunting task of sorting and delivering millions of backlogged letters and packages to troops in the European Theater.

Ten of the women of the 6888th were Missourians, including two St. Louisans. One of the two was Army Tech 4 Pearline McKell. Pearline's family lived on Cote Brilliante Avenue in North St. Louis with her parents and three siblings. She and her mother worked as hotel maids in the years before the war. In 1943, Pearline joined the Women's Army Auxiliary Corps, (WAAC). She was assigned to duty at Walla Walla Army Air Field in Washington State as a clerk typist before entering the postal unit. Soon, she and the other women of the "Six Triple Eight" were given a monumental task.

The 6888th arrived in Birmingham, England, in 1945 and found warehouses filled with undelivered mail—some of it sitting for months. Many of the letters lacked full addresses or contained misspellings, requiring the women of the unit to create an extensive directory of military personnel. They worked tirelessly in shifts around the clock, sorting an average of 65,000 pieces of mail per shift. Thanks to their dedication, they cleared a six-month backlog in just three months, ensuring that troops received their long-awaited messages from home.

The importance of their work cannot be overstated. As important as any soldier on the battlefield, they kept the war effort moving forward. Despite facing discrimination both abroad and at home, the woman of the 6888th persevered, knowing that their mission was essential to maintaining morale. Their motto, "No Mail, Low Morale," reflected their understanding of just how vital letters were to those on the front lines.

For the soldiers and sailors who grew up on The Hill, in The Ville, South City, Kirkwood, Ferguson, or across the rivers in

East St. Louis or St. Charles, or in any of the neighborhoods and communities of the Gateway region, a letter bearing a postmark from their hometown was a true gift. Despite censorship and postal challenges, letters remained a crucial connection between home and the battlefield, bridging distances and sustaining hope.

Downtown St. Louis, 1930s. *Collections of the Missouri Historical Society*

ST. LOUIS BEFORE THE OUTBREAK OF WAR

Before Congress enacted the Uniform Monday Holiday Act in 1968, Memorial Day was celebrated on May 31 rather than being observed on the last Monday in May as it is today. In 1941, May 31 fell on a Friday, making it a three-day weekend. With three solid days of no work at their disposal, getting a jump on summer fun was the primary objective for many St. Louisans that Memorial Day weekend. Their minds were on fun, relaxation, and shaking off the last trappings of cabin fever after a long winter and rainy spring cooped up at home or in offices and factories. Thousands packed up the family car and headed out of town, away from the traffic and smog that characterized the city. The roads quickly filled with travelers destined for the fishing and recreational resorts along the Meramec River and other tourist playgrounds of the Ozarks. By Thursday evening, the Missouri Highway Patrol reported traffic was "exceedingly heavy," and by

Saturday morning, noted the *Globe-Democrat*, "St. Louis motorists were scattered at resorts, homes of country relatives, and in other cities hundreds of miles away."

Those who stayed behind headed to the parks or the neighborhood public pools, which were now open for the season. "The city and county parks," the *Globe* continued, "were crowded with those on picnics and others engaged in games on the sports fields." The thought that this might be the last summer of normalcy for many years was hardly on the minds of those enjoying the fresh air, green grass, and sunshine. Yes, the news from abroad was chilling, but those problems seemed too distant to be of any genuine concern. St. Louisans, like most Americans, went about with little fear that their lives would soon drastically change.

Not everyone hit the highways. Many did choose to stay home, and of the thousands who remained, many took time to remember Memorial Day's true purpose: remembering those who had fought and died in America's previous wars.

Only five years earlier, President Roosevelt had dedicated the opening of the Soldiers Memorial on Market Street, a monument to those St. Louisans who had made the ultimate sacrifice during World War I. Now on this Memorial Day, 1941, a few thousand St. Louisans gathered to participate in the formal observances organized by the St. Louis chapter of the Disabled American Veterans of the World War (DAVWW), the precursor to today's Disabled American Veterans. For the ceremony, the DAVWW erected an enormous white cross at the top of the Memorial staircase, which, on that bright May morning, cast a shadow upon the polished limestone steps and further added to the sense that this was a sacred space. The cross's presence hearkened to the smaller crosses adorning the graves of St. Louisans buried thousands of miles away in France, those men who died in the nightmarish trenches and muddy, barbed wire fields of the Great War.

In the quiet loggia of the Memorial, a marble cenotaph bears the names of those men. On that sunny yet somber Memorial

Day, many families and friends undoubtedly searched for the names inscribed on that symbolic tomb for their son, father, or brother. One can only imagine that seeing the names recalled the pain loved ones felt when they learned of their loss, possibly mixed with a sense of pride in believing that these soldiers had died to usher in a new era of peace and bring to completion the "war to end all wars."

In the tradition of memorial observances, patriotic music played on this morning, and dignitaries read speeches; then, as the ceremony concluded, the crowd fell silent as a soldier standing near the enormous cenotaph sounded taps. His notes reverberated through the crowd and down the corridor of buildings lining Market Street. At the same time, a second trumpeter sounded in reply from the steps of the Municipal Courts Building, a mournful tribute to the fallen.

On that same day, south of the city at Jefferson Barracks Military Post, a crowd of 3,000 spectators watched as 4,000 recruits, led by the post band, paraded across the grounds to the speaker's stand in the National Cemetery. The rousing marches of John Philip Sousa drifted over row upon row of white headstones. These individual markers reminded all of the costs of war and the honor of those who had served before most of these recruits were born.

In attendance that morning, sitting near the reviewing stand, were representatives of various veterans' groups, including two surviving veterans of the Civil War. Of all the speakers, the most prophetic and impassioned speech came from Army Colonel S. B. Philpot, retired commanding officer of Jefferson Barracks, who used his platform to warn the crowd of the rising war clouds and America's need to prepare for what lay ahead.

As an old soldier who had endured the horrors of war in the trenches of World War I, and who, from experience, recognized the signs of growing danger, the colonel urged those St. Louisans gathered around him to take heed. Philpot spelled it out. "This country faces its worst crisis since the civil war," he said, noting,

"It's time for America to start praying." He urged those listening that morning to consider how different the circumstances were in Europe today compared to the situations among America's allies in 1917. When the US entered the Great War, Russia, Italy, the Balkan states, and France stood allied with America to repel the Germans, but the Europe of 1941 was a very different place. Those former allies were now either neutralized by Hitler's ever-expanding blitzkrieg across Europe or stood with him as part of the Axis powers. England, the colonel decried, "is upholding democracy alone, and she has her back to the wall." America, Philpot stressed, "must do everything she can to assist her."

While most Americans did not feel that the US should enter the war in Europe, Hitler's unbridled lust for land and power was not going unnoticed. Public anxiety about a direct threat to the United States by Germany was slowly rising. Those 4,000 recruits who stood on the parade ground at Jefferson Barracks on Memorial Day were newly drafted men who had been called up under the new Selective Training and Service Act. The president signed the Burke–Wadsworth Act into law in September 1940, and there was little public resistance to the first peacetime draft. Most Americans generally accepted that they should be prepared for the worst.

Public opinion also was leaning toward more direct intervention

Jefferson Barracks, 1930s. *Collections of the Missouri Historical Society*

to assist Great Britain. Only two months before Philpot's address at Jefferson Barracks, Congress passed President Roosevelt's Lend-Lease Act, allowing the United States to supply Great Britain with ships, military equipment, and other armaments to defend itself from Germany's onslaught. Roosevelt's indirect means of helping our ally while maintaining a certain degree of neutrality was well-received by the public. For many St. Louisans, that level of support for supplying our allies with equipment and provisions to resist Nazi aggression was likely tempered by a certain degree of fear that we could be pulled into the conflict, but the city's workers and community leaders were also reaping the economic benefits of building our national defenses and supplying our allies with military hardware. The Lend-Lease program and the US government's new focus on military preparedness opened the door for increased production of planes, bullets, shells, and other defense products produced within the new factories rising in and around St. Louis.

Curtiss-Wright was among the first corporations to benefit from the massive defense build-up. The company had a facility at Lambert Field producing transport aircraft that employed 1,500 workers, and in October 1940, Curtiss-Wright's President Guy Vaugh and Vice President C. W. France announced the construction of a new $10 million factory located on 14 acres of land adjacent to the airport. The final facility would be seven times the size of the existing plant and employ 8,000 workers. Furthermore, Curtiss-Wright would rent several other Bridgeton and St. Louis buildings to accommodate engineering offices and storage spaces. It was the kind of news that overjoyed city officials.

At the end of 1940, the city received more good news. The Western Cartridge Company purchased 133 acres along Bircher and Goodfellow Streets to build a $28 million small arms munitions plant operated under the supervision of the War Department. The factory would employ 5,000 to 6,000 workers but could expand to 8,000 to 10,000 with increased production. Meanwhile, existing businesses such as Busch-Sulzer Brothers Diesel Engine Company, a sideline of Anheuser-Busch that produced engines for the Navy's submarine fleet, kicked into high gear to meet production quotas.

It was encouraging news for workers still recovering from the hardships of the Great Depression. Thousands of new jobs were created with each new defense plant, ironically providing hope for a better life for those who had suffered during the lean years.

Defense production became one of the city's largest industries, and more so after the war began. Automobile and train car factories switched assembly lines to produce tanks and armored vehicles. Clothing companies turned from manufacturing dress shirts and dresses to producing uniforms and helmet covers. The city's shoe manufacturers switched from making ladies' pumps to men's Army boots. The American Stove Company converted to manufacturing shells and ammunition. St. Louis's industrial output pivoted nearly overnight as government defense contracts changed the direction of many of the region's businesses.

The workforce also changed with the coming of the war. The image of Rosie the Riveter has become synonymous with wartime production in America, and the factories of St. Louis were no exception in hiring a large workforce of local women. Women as part of the factory workforce was nothing new in St. Louis since the garment factories had employed large numbers for decades, but heavy production jobs were something different. In August 1942, the *St. Louis Globe-Democrat* addressed the phenomenon of women in war production plants under the headline, "Wheel of Fate Spins, Throws These Girls from Civilian Jobs to War Jobs." The article showcased six women working at the Curtiss-Wright plant at Lambert Field. Under the slogan "Keep 'Em Flying," they built the aircraft soon to be shuttling troops and dive-bombing targets. Their previous work included everything from performing at the St. Louis Opera to working in shoe factories and being a stenographer for a bookstore.

Curtiss-Wright was just one of many factories that welcomed women once the male workforce was constricted by the draft and

Curtiss-Wright assembly floor, Lambert Field. *Collections of the Missouri Historical Society*

enlistments. The work was hard, but the pay was generally good. Each of the women interviewed by the *Globe* expressed satisfaction in her job and that she was contributing to the victory effort. But of drill press operator Doris Holmes the newspaper wrote, "She likes this sort of work and expects to continue in industry, war or no war, and that men will find displacing a skilled worker such as herself quite a task." Such sentiments among the women were not uncommon, but when the war was over, many were displaced and had to return to less skilled work. However, the seeds were planted for an expanded role of women in the workforce, and the times were changing.

While women were taking their place in the working world, another group also filled a need and gained work. Disabled workers began to fill jobs and prove that they could contribute, "winning the approval of even the most skeptical employers," reported the *Globe-Democrat* in 1942. As many as 2,300 people with disabilities had found work in textile factories and defense plants. Besides demonstrating that people with disabilities were more than capable of holding down regular, daily jobs, they also were viewed as models for those wounded soldiers who would be returning home after the war and seeking employment. C. Walter Placke, the director of the US Employment Service, was quoted as saying, "The handicapped worker today is teaching employers that a man's worth on the job is not measured by what he cannot do, but what he can still do as well or better than others."

With the factories operating at full capacity and the workforce focused on producing the equipment and goods to win the war, St. Louis was an industrial powerhouse. With money again in people's pockets and the determination to get the job done, St. Louisans' hopes were high, and victory was only a matter of time.

Curtiss-Wright assembly floor, Lambert Field. *Collections of the Missouri Historical Society*

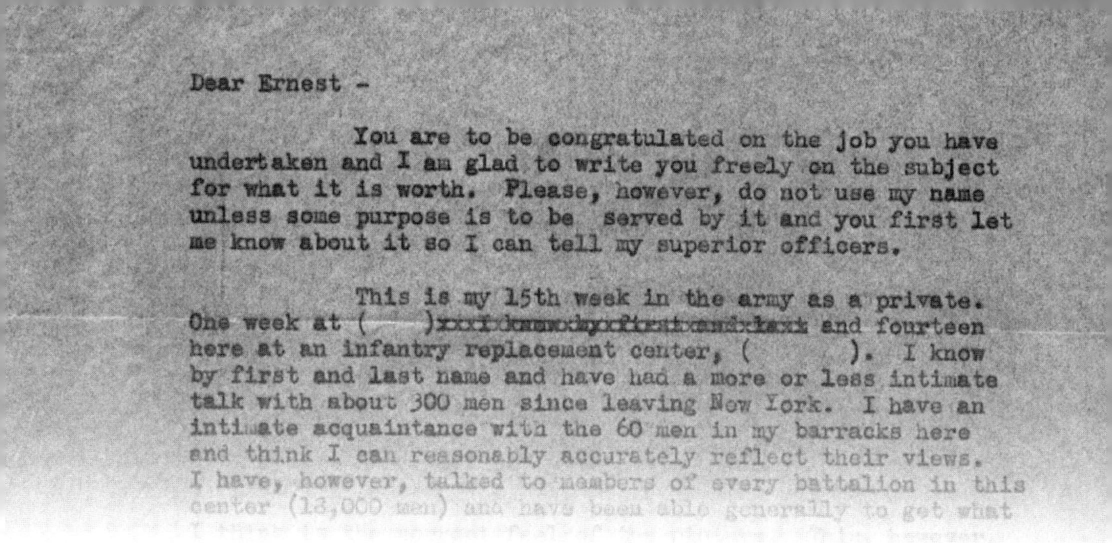
Dear Ernest -

You are to be congratulated on the job you have undertaken and I am glad to write you freely on the subject for what it is worth. Please, however, do not use my name unless some purpose is to be served by it and you first let me know about it so I can tell my superior officers.

This is my 15th week in the army as a private. One week at ( ) ~~xxxxxxxxxxxxxxxxxxxxxxxx~~ and fourteen here at an infantry replacement center, ( ). I know by first and last name and have had a more or less intimate talk with about 300 men since leaving New York. I have an intimate acquaintance with the 60 men in my barracks here and think I can reasonably accurately reflect their views. I have, however, talked to members of every battalion in this center (18,000 men) and have been able generally to get what

Private William McChesney Martin letter, July 25, 1941. *Collections of the Missouri Historical Society*

"THERE IS NO QUESTION IN MY MIND (EVEN UNDER OUR PRESENT INEFFICIENT MILITARY PROCEDURE) WE CAN AND WILL WIN THE WAR."

— PRIVATE WILLIAM MCCHESNEY MARTIN, US ARMY

The peacetime draft enacted in 1940 required all male citizens aged 21–35 to register for selective service. Local draft boards were established across the nation to oversee the selection process and notify men when their assigned draft number had been drawn according to a national lottery. There was a process for exceptions based on circumstances such as health, critical occupations, or being an enrolled student, but beyond that men who fell within the age range were obligated to serve.

Given the older age range of those required to register, many of the first draftees were men who were not only married family men but also established in their occupations. It was a major disruption for most who had no choice but to report and serve. The law established a mandatory 12-month term of duty with an additional 10 years of reserve service once discharged from regular service. A 34-year-old married father of two might find himself struggling through boot camp alongside some unmarried 22-year-old. These conditions created a certain degree of resentment among the older inductees and did not translate into good morale among the troops.

While the selection process was created to be totally democratic, many tried to use various channels of privilege to get exemptions from service, and when those who could avoid service did so, it generated resentment among those who did not have the clout. Yet, there was one privileged young man from St. Louis who not only chose to not avoid service but also took his turn in part to prove a point that all men regardless of their status should serve when called.

William McChesney Martin, known to most as Bill, was drafted in the spring of 1941. Given Martin's position as the head of the New York Stock Exchange, such a circumstance was hardly an everyday event. But he was still of service age and unwilling to use any possible political connections to skirt his duty to his country. Needless to say, the press loved it and followed Martin's journey all the way through the induction and training process.

As a native St. Louisan, Martin's sudden introduction to Army life was of particular interest to the city's newspapers. As the son of one of the city's most prominent financial leaders, William

McChesney Martin Sr., a governor of the Federal Reserve Bank of St. Louis and one of the founders of the Federal Reserve system, young Bill did not grow up like most of the other draftees. He attended the private Country Day School and later entered Yale, where he studied English. After graduation, young Martin worked for the Federal Reserve then became the head of statistics for A. G. Edwards & Sons.

In February 1941, Martin was living in New York City and working on Wall Street when he received his draft notice in the mail. A press release followed in which Martin announced his willingness to serve because he did not believe anyone, regardless of their position, should ignore the call of service to their county. Martin told General Lewis Hershey, the head of the Selective Service, that he would not seek an exemption as a way of showing that the draft should reflect men of all capabilities. Like the others, Martin reported for duty and took his place as a private in the United States Army. A nationally circulated photograph at the time of Martin's induction shows him being fingerprinted with the other new inductees at the New York processing center with the headline "Martin gets $47,676 Wage Cut," noting that his new monthly pay as a private was $324, a significant reduction from his $48,000 annual salary as head of the Exchange.

Although Martin was a private and assigned as a general clerk, he certainly had more influence than the average GI. As he made his way through basic training and took on his duties at Fort Dix, Martin made it a point to observe his fellow inductees and get a better understanding of the attitudes and morale of the men. What he saw concerned him. Martin had little doubt that America would soon be entering the war, yet based on his experiences, he felt that the men seemed indifferent, ill informed, and unmotivated for the challenges ahead. He expressed his concerns to his friend Ernest Angell, who was a founding member of the newly established Council for Democracy, an organization established to largely counter much of the isolationist rhetoric being circulated by

America First, a highly visible group of American business leaders, politicians, and others like famed American flyer Charles Lindbergh who actively rallied against American involvement in the war.

The Council for Democracy feared for the future of democracy in Europe and the growing threat of fascist organizations in the United States. At the time Martin wrote the following long assessment in the form of a letter to Angell, who by then was serving as the president of the Council for Democracy. Martin's descriptions of the soldiers with whom he served paint a picture of an Army composed of men who needed to better understand the threat to America posed by Hitler and the world's other despots. Particularly disturbing are his comments concerning the plight of the German Jews and the general indifference felt by some of the men concerning this issue.

Private Martin offers not only his insights but also his suggestions to improve the men's morale and to educate the men on their purpose in serving in the military. They needed not only instruction in civics but also a more pronounced infusion of good ole American patriotism, including flags and military bands.

Martin did not have much faith in the officers whom he encountered, either. There was, in his opinion, a clear lack of good military minds in charge and good role models for the soldiers to learn from. Nevertheless, Martin clearly had faith in the general American fighting man. Given the right instruction and tools, he felt they would all make fine soldiers.

July 25, 1941

Dear Ernest—

You are to be congratulated on the job you have undertaken and I am glad to write you freely on the subject for what it is worth. Please, however, do not use my name unless some purpose is to be served by it and you first let me know about it so I can tell my superior officers.

This is my 15th week in the army as a private. One week at

[self censored] and fourteen here at an infantry placement center, [self censored]. I know by first and last name and have had a more or less intimate talk with about 300 men since leaving New York. I have an intimate acquaintance with the 60 men in my barracks here and think I can reasonably accurately reflect their views. I have, however, talked to members of every battalion in the center (18,000 men) and have been able to generally get what I think is the correct feel of the picture. This, however, is just one small cross section of the army and it may by *no means be typical*. Since induction all my spare time has been spent in Gallup polls of my own and thinking on what effect this all will have on the future of this country—most of it has been directed towards a study of the distinction between morale and discipline in a military sense but enough of it applies to your interests to warrant comment. I give you this background so you will know my qualifications and limitations as a commentator in this field.

Major conclusions to date: (1) the morale of the draftee is low but on the whole a lot better than one would expect when the drastic change is considered objectively. Lives have been completely disrupted, futures blighted, prospective homes destroyed and in addition few people are happy at first when they change anything (I remember personally it took me six months to get to stand Wall Street after moving there from Saint Louis). Defined American trait of "I can take it" shines through all of this and the attitude of the man in the ranks is on the whole good. They *do not understand* what it is all about but they would like to learn and a great opportunity to sell them worthwhile values in which they instinctively believe now, because they are Americans, but are beginning to doubt, presents itself.

(2) Morale in the readjustment sense tends to improve with time not as fast as it normally should but the trend is in the right direction, but morale in an ideological or political or psychological sense starts declining and here at least with minor interruptions the trend is alarmingly

down. *The leadership in the army is second rate* compared to the attitude and, in the case of a great many selectees, the training and ability of the men. *Leadership is badly needed* in this sense (some of the military men at the top like my Commanding General [self censored]) are very able and intelligent men but there are not enough of his stripe and his job is primarily military anyhow and some excellent military men are handicapped by their training along purely military lines from understanding the psychology of a selectee. There is no question in my mind (even under our present inefficient military procedure) we can and will win the war. Unless leadership develops to improve the situation I seriously question whether the freedom for which we are basically struggling will be attained. Hitler may well win a moral victory even though losing in a military sense. In fact the trend here is to destroy subconscious faith in free institutions because of the overlapping of military discipline (necessary but unexplained) end the stupidity of what the men (many of whom are quite able even if not university graduates) laughingly call "our leaders."

Minor conclusions: answers to your questions:

1. The average soldier has little idea of why he has been drafted and a lot are suspicious of the whole move. The older men 30–35 are inclined to be bitter about mistakes of their draft boards and all know some men much younger than themselves and in less important jobs whose numbers have not come up and who they feel should have been taken first. This is an aside but in my judgment as one of that number they have a good grievance.

2. Only one in five or six has any faith in the belief there is a crisis or a threat to democracy in the sense of loss of freedom to them individually or their friends. Their knowledge of democracy is almost nil. Our army as seen here is not becoming a fighting army in the psychological sense. The only point about Germany fully understood is persecution of the Jews and needless to say not everyone thinks that is so bad.

I could give you some interesting excerpts from my diary on actual straw votes it has been my pleasure to take but the conclusions would only be strengthened and it is too hard to do much writing as a private in the army where you only have the foot of your bed and some borrowed stationary like this.

Concrete proposals for improvement: based again on that goes on in the little orbit I see.

1. I have only seen the American flag once—and that on a parade here. We don't have enough bands. Enough of the things which would subconsciously stir patriotism. We need from Washington conscience, unashamed, honest morale building steps. We need to be told as soldiers what a privilege it is to wear the uniform as an offset to a lot of the crushed pride the military life requires.

2. The issuance of a booklet of some sort available to every man giving in general terms the purpose of our army, National Defense, etcetera, necessity for military discipline. We need an honest, fearless, intelligent war department directed drive to teach the meaning of our constitution etcetera.

3. Out of these two previous points, actually the game, must come a recognition of younger men of merit in the army, a conviction they are not being discriminated against because they are selectees (a feeling a lot of them including myself sometimes have) that there will be a future based on merit and a minimum of economic waste and that democracy is functioning and not just a stupid dogma all men are created equal when we see proof on all sides they are not equal. It is naturally difficult to write this way under the handicap of a camp life but the general idea of what you want is here. I am going to finish my training period here this week and then go to [self censored] the 1st of next week. If this is useful to you you might ask your secretary to make a couple of copies and send it to me for amplification and editing, if not it was fun writing anyhow.

Give my best to Mrs. Angell.

As ever,

Bill Martin

This letter exemplifies the level of analysis that Martin invested in any project or topic he pursued. Being a mover and shaker in the financial world certainly gave Private Martin a leg up over the average soldier, but his skills, knowledge, and abilities largely allowed him to advance throughout his military career. It was not long into his new Army career that he caught the attention of General Hap Arnold of the US Army Air Corps, who appointed Martin to his general staff. By the time the war ended, Private Martin was a full colonel. He had climbed the ladder quickly from a clerical clerk to one of the military command's most trusted senior advisors. He played a prominent role in maintaining the delicate balance of the US and Soviet relations through his work with the lend-lease program, and near the end of the war President Harry S. Truman appointed him to head the Export-Import Bank of the United States. This entity financed the production of war materials for Allied nations.

Upon leaving the military in 1946, Martin continued his public service by serving as assistant secretary of the Treasury in the Truman administration. From there he went on to hold one of the country's most powerful finance positions. In 1951, President Truman appointed him chairman of the Federal Reserve. He served under five presidents and holds the distinction of being the longest-serving chair of the Fed before retiring in 1970. He is buried in Bellefontaine Cemetery in St. Louis.

'WHAT'S THIS?'

—ASSOCIATED PRESS WIREPHOTO

WASHINGTON, August 13.—Private William McChesney Martin Jr., 34-year-old former president of the New York Stock Exchange, scratches his head as he looks over the signs on a building at the Army War College where he reported for duty today as a clerk with a quartermaster detachment. He was assigned to general clerical work.

William McChesney Martin, who served as president of the New York Stock Exchange, was drafted in 1941. He entered the Army with the rank of private with the belief that he did not deserve special treatment or deferment. *Newspapers.com*

Fire and smoke billow from the wreckage of the USS *Arizona* on December 7, 1941. *National Archives*

ST. LOUISANS AT WAR

On the evening of December 7, 1941, young servicemen gathered in downtown St. Louis at Municipal Auditorium (today's Stifel Theatre) to attend the dance regularly hosted by the USO for local military personnel. Despite the harrowing events of that morning, the USO dance went on as usual, perhaps as a way of projecting some degree of normalcy to an otherwise horrific day. Typically, these dances were alive with young men and women cutting the dance floor to Benny Goodman songs belted out by the USO band, but on this night, no one was in the mood to dance. "Soldiers and hostesses were grim-faced," observed a reporter from the *Globe-Democrat*. Rather than socializing as usual, those in attendance were mostly gathered in small groups reading the *Globe-Democrat*'s extra edition printed to provide the latest news coming from Pearl Harbor. The young men and women in attendance that night all understood there was no further question of whether we were going to war. The United States was not about to let this attack go unchecked, and it would now be their job to do the fighting.

The attack seemed to come as no surprise to the servicemen attending the dance. As active members of the military, they, more than anyone, were in the position to hear from their superiors the likelihood of America joining the war. The *Globe* reporter noted that the young soldiers and sailors that night met the news with a "spirit of fatalism." The general feeling expressed was that there was now a job to do, and it was best to finish what the Japanese had started. Yet, no doubt these young men knew that this was going to be neither a quick nor easy job. "I've been waiting and expecting this a long time," one sailor told the reporter. "I guess we'll have to get it over with." A similar sense of resigned duty was expressed by two other soldiers playing a game of Chinese checkers to pass the time. "We might as well get in and get it over with," they remarked.

Another serviceman, a soldier, told the reporter he heard of the attack and Japan's declaration of war on America while he was eating lunch. "Boy, it kinda ruined that meal," he said. "I'm sorry to hear it, but I guess what has to be has to be."

While the servicemen at the dance understood and accepted that they were now charged with fighting a war a long way from home, the civilian populations feared that the attack on Pearl Harbor, an American base located within an American territory, might result in direct attacks on cities like Los Angeles, San Francisco, or New York. At the USO dance, a hostess was asked why she appeared so glum. "Well, my fiancé is on the Pacific Coast," she told the reporter. The young hostess possessed an anxiety that many Americans held in those early months after Pearl Harbor, that Japan's use of aircraft carriers and submarines allowed them a reach perhaps far enough to attack not just the West Coast but anywhere in the continental United States.

The general anxiety that any place could be a target and vulnerable to attack was evident in the immediate action of Missouri Governor Phil Donnelly and St. Louis city officials, who ordered police units to guard defense plants. In St. Louis County, a defense council was organized by county officials. The volunteer unit consisted of "farmers with squirrel rifles and shotguns," reported the *Globe-Democrat*. These unlikely minutemen were sworn in as deputy sheriffs to guard the bridges on Highway 40 between St. Louis and Columbia.

The magnitude of the Pearl Harbor and Manila attacks became even more evident when word of the deaths of St. Louis servicemen serving aboard Navy ships in the harbor or stationed at the bases at Hickam Field and Manila began to trickle back to local residents. Word of the first Missourian killed in the attack was released in an Associated Press wire story on December 9. The victim was Second Lieutenant George A. Whiteman of Sedalia, Missouri, a member of the US Army Air Corps. Whiteman's name is now familiar to many. Fourteen years after his death, Whiteman's sacrifice was honored with the renaming of Sedalia Air Force Base as Whiteman Air Force Base.

St. Louisans learned of the first city resident to die in the attack on December 11, when it was announced that Private Robert H. Westbrook Jr., a radio operator and member of the 26th Bomber Squadron based at Hickam Field, had been killed

Bridges in St. Louis County were guarded against possible sabotage. A soldier stands guard at the Daniel Boone Bridge over the Missouri River between St. Louis and St. Charles County. *Collections of the Missouri Historical Society*

in the attack. Westbrook attended Shenandoah School and St. Margaret of Scotland Parish during his years in St. Louis. He was a neighborhood kid like so many others in the city, and his death likely drove home the notion that other sad announcements would soon follow.

Over the next days and weeks, reports of more St. Louis casualties began to circulate as the War Department released the names of those who were verified as killed in action during the attack. Others were reported missing among the 18 Navy ships sunk in the harbor. Among the sailors reported missing was Paul Boemer, a crewman aboard the USS *Oklahoma*, which was moored on Battleship Row in the harbor. The *Oklahoma* was a prime target for the Japanese dive-bombers, and she was slammed with eight torpedoes within the first 10 minutes of the attack. The sudden and violent strike made it difficult for her sailors to escape and abandon ship as the *Oklahoma* quickly sank into the mud. She lost 429 of her men that morning, many of whom were trapped inside the sinking battleship. Boemer was one of the unlucky caught inside. When the bodies of the dead were finally recovered, only 35 could be identified. Boemer was among the unknowns. However, the Navy never forgot these men nor abandoned their effort to identify them. Eighty years later, DNA testing would confirm Boemer's remains, and he was finally brought home to St. Louis to be put to rest in his hometown.

The jarring news of the attack instilled more than just fear, unfortunately; it also erupted in misdirected anger and hate. Within days of the attacks, local businesses reported that they were removing all goods marked "Made in Japan" for fear of retribution. They were taking no chances given the level of anti-Japanese feelings.

But more suspicion was directed against those who might have any ties to the Japanese government, no matter how mundane. Immediately after news of the Japanese attack was received, state and local officials turned their attention to rounding up Japanese residents whom they suspected of being sympathetic to Japanese aggression. Governor Donnelly issued an executive order for the house arrest of any non-naturalized Japanese persons living in Missouri. Around 50 St. Louisans of Japanese descent were identified and cleared, but the risk of arrest went beyond the actions of state authorities. Within hours of the Pearl Harbor attack, St. Louis resident Tetsu Uyeda, a 20-year resident of the city, was detained by the FBI. Uyeda was the well-known manager of the exclusive Bridlespur Hunt Club, but he also served as the local Japan Tourism Bureau representative. As a registered agent of the Japanese government, he was viewed, as one federal agent noted, as "potentially dangerous." However, Uyeda was never charged with espionage, nor was evidence ever found that he had participated in any illegal activity. Nevertheless he was sent to a Japanese internment camp in New Mexico.

Uyeda's family, with help from several prominent St. Louisans, submitted petitions to the Enemy Alien Board to plead for his release, but all attempts to bring him home were ignored. He was detained for the duration of the war.

It was clear that St. Louisans, even those who had initially protested US involvement, rallied to support the war effort. The city's patriotism was evident, and the people were united in the cause to defend their country and defeat fascism. The pain of Pearl Harbor and Manila was sobering, and the reality of once again sending American boys overseas to fight was a hard pill to swallow, but the long lines of young men who gathered at local recruiting centers was a testament to the belief that America could no longer stand by quietly while the rest of the world was in flames and the enemies were at the gates.

To the relief of many St. Louis families, letters from loved ones who had survived the attacks in Hawaii and elsewhere began to trickle back home. The sense of relief that these letters provided were a godsend to those who waited in hopes of knowing that their sons, brothers, or husbands were alive and safe. Besides providing assurance, hearing their stories instilled pride and reinforced the need to support the daunting cause that lay ahead.

News from Our Detroit Branch

Tommy McLogan F. M. Rodgers, III

Mrs. Dorothy Royce Grable, Receptionist at our Detroit Branch, has volunteered to keep us informed regarding Wagner employees in Detroit, and here is her first news release.

Norman Andrews Is File and Locator Clerk in Army Personnel Office

His Brother Norman Was Cited for Bravery at Pearl Harbor

Alphonse Andrews Norman Andrews

Maceo Cole (Dept. 23) has passed on to the Editor a letter he received from Norman A. Andrews, who left his job of order filler in the Packing and Shipping Department on March 24 to answer his Country's call. In the letter, written on May 24 we find:

Hello Maceo:

Well, how are you and all of the gang at Wagner now? Tell all of them that I said Hello, and keep in there and fight. I think I will be back to see them around the latter part of September, when my first furlough is due. Tell Mr. Murphy and Mr. Harvey that I said it's not so bad to be in the Army after all. Tell the gang, Maceo, that I'm a File and Locator Clerk in the Personnel Office. It's a very fine, clean job.

I remain as ever,

PVT. NORMAN A. ANDREWS.

United States Army, Group II Personnel Office, Fort Belvoir, Va.

Norman has a brother, Alphonse, who was in Pearl Harbor on December 7, and who wrote to Pervis Smith (Dept. 17) on January 20:

Well, I guess since I left I have been laughed at with the old "I told you so," but let me say that I know of no other place that I'd rather be than here at the present time. We bore the brunt of the first attack very well, and I was right in the middle of it. It was an experience I shall never forget. It was a savage attack, but once we obtain strategic points of advantage, this war with the Japs won't last long.

What Alphonse Andrews was too modest to tell us was that he was cited for bravery under fire. Like a true American, he disregarded the fact that as one in civilian attire he could have dashed for cover, but instead he carried on his work for the U. S. Navy even tho bombs were creating chaos and killing people all about him.

BUY WAR BONDS AND WAR STAMPS

L. E. James' Unit Ready for Service

now; we had a written commendation from Lt. Gen. Arnold, Commander of the Army Air Forces, the other day, saying that we were the first

dled before, but has the responsibility storing a larger amount and a far gre er variety of material. Just the item 37 mm. shot steel alone involves a c siderable tonnage (actual volume a m tary secret). And never before has th been such a record-breaking volume sheet steel for motors, transformers, a truck brake shoes. And Reporter Moore of the same department adds t Department 98 is safety-conscious, a that it is keeping its lost-time accid record clean.

BUY WAR BONDS

Jane Dachroeden Collects Scr Rubber

This is a war in which every m woman, and child must take part if V tory is to be attain In fact, this w means far more the youngsters tha does to the adults, *they* are the ones Axis has the b chance of enslavi *they* are the ones t will be impoverish underfed, and in g eral abused by t racketeers of G many, Italy, and pan. It is *their* fut we at Wagner and the Armed Forces fighting to protect, that *they* too may enjoy life, liberty, the pursuit of happiness their pare enjoyed.

Jane Dachroeden, age 6, daughter George Dachroeden (Building 18), fully conscious of the fact that this is

Wagner Election Victory News, June 1942. *Collections of the Missouri Historical Society*

"I KNOW OF NO OTHER PLACE THAT I'D RATHER BE THAN HERE AT THE PRESENT TIME."
— ALPHONSE A. ANDREWS, US NAVY CANTONMENT CHAUFFEUR

Alphonse A. Andrews, a civilian worker for the US Navy Cantonment at Pearl Harbor, epitomizes the steadfast spirit and patriotic resolve of countless Americans who faced the brutal attack on December 7, 1941. His actions that day, alongside the profound historical context of the assault, underscore the strength and resilience that defined the American response during the darkest hours of World War II.

Born in Magnolia, Mississippi, in 1910, Alphonse was one of eight children of Francis and Ginny Andrews. In Mississippi, Francis worked in a sawmill, but like many African Americans of his time, he wanted a better life beyond the oppressive confines of the segregated South. The Andrews family sought to improve their lot in life by moving north to St. Louis in 1923.

From their family home on Cora Street, the Andrews children attended Sumner High School. Alphonse's sister, Dorris, became a teacher and another, Vernice, became a photographer. His little brother, Norman, was elected Sumner class president before working for Wagner Electric upon completing school. Alphonse too sought to improve his position and attended Harris-Stowe College. But the Depression years were difficult, and Alphonse did not complete his degree. He found work as a chauffeur for the Raith family in Clayton and spent nine years in their employment before leaving to join his brother at the Wagner Electric factory in Wellston.

In the fall of 1941, Alphonse heard that the US Navy needed civilian workers, particularly chauffeurs to drive trucks and staff cars at the Navy Yards in Hawaii. The pay was good, and moving to Hawaii was an exciting prospect. In October 1941, Alphonse was hired, and he found himself bound for Pearl Harbor aboard the USS *Wharton* sailing out of San Francisco. Little did he know that this fateful journey would thrust him into one of the most pivotal moments in American history.

On the morning of December 7, 1941, as Japanese aircraft swooped down on the US naval base in Hawaii, the world changed forever. The surprise attack by the Empire of Japan, which aimed to cripple the US Pacific Fleet, devastated Pearl Harbor, causing widespread destruction and loss of life. As bombs rained down and gunfire echoed across the harbor, Alphonse Andrews, though a civilian, found himself amidst the chaos, working at the heart of the Navy's operations.

In a letter dated January 20, 1941, Alphonse wrote to his friend, Pervis Smith, recounting his experience amidst the harrowing assault.

The letter was submitted by Smith, who worked at Wagner Electric, to the editors of the *Victory News*, a company newsletter that allowed employees to learn firsthand about St. Louisans serving and fighting.

> January 20, 1942
>
> Well, I guess since I left I have been laughed at with the old 'I told you so,' but let me say that I know of no other place that I'd rather be than here at the present time. We bore the brunt of the first attack very well, and I was right in the middle of it. It was an experience I shall never forget. It was a savage attack, but once we obtain strategic points of advantage, this war with the Japs won't last long.
>
> Adolphus

His words, brimming with confidence and unshaken resolve, captured not only the immediacy of the moment but also the unwavering determination that would define America's fight during the war. Despite the overwhelming odds, Alphonse continued his work in the face of danger, exemplifying bravery under fire. While chaos unfolded around him, he remained committed to his mission, embodying the valor that would propel the nation to victory.

The editor of the Wagner newsletter added, "What Alphonse was too modest to tell us was that he was cited for bravery under fire. Like a true American, he disregarded the fact that as one in civilian attire he could have dashed for cover, but instead he carried on his work for the US Navy even tho bombs were creating chaos and killing people all about him."

In March 1942, Admiral C. C. Bloch, commandant of the Fourteenth Naval District, awarded a citation to Alphonse Andrews and his coworkers in the transportation department for "most efficient action and unusual presence of mind on your part . . . during the attack on the Fleet in Pearl Harbor, Territory of Hawaii, by Japanese forces on December 7 1941 in handling all emergencies or rescue work that came to your attention in a calm, cool, and outstanding manner."

Norman Andrews Is File and Locator Clerk in Army Personnel Office

His Brother Norman Was Cited for Bravery at Pearl Harbor

Alphonse Andrews | Norman Andrews

The Andrews brothers worked for Wagner Electric prior to the war. Alphonse (left) was a civilian Navy worker at Pearl Harbor at the time of the attack. Norman became a staff sergeant in the Army and served stateside during the war. *Collections of the Missouri Historical Society*

Alphonse's courage was not an isolated act. His brother, Norman, also answered the call of duty, serving in the Army during World War II, contributing to the collective effort of the Andrews family in support of the war effort. Norman mustered out of the Army as a staff sergeant at the war's end. He joined the St. Louis Metropolitan Police Department in 1946 and gained a reputation as a no-nonsense patrolman. The Andrews family, like so many others, played their part in defeating those who threatened peace and freedom at home and abroad. Alphonse's bravery at Pearl Harbor speaks volumes about the resilience and determination of those who fought, whether on the battlefield or in the workplace.

In the face of a savage attack, Alphonse did not flinch. His actions at Pearl Harbor remain a testament to the spirit of all those who rose to meet the challenges of the war, reminding us of the sacrifices made and the unyielding strength of the American people during one of history's most trying times.

Alphonse continued to work at the Navy Yards in Pearl Harbor until 1946, when he resigned due to health reasons. He returned home to St. Louis and had a long career with the United States Postal Service. He is buried in north St. Louis County. Norman is buried in Jefferson Barracks National Cemetery.

FORT SILL, OKLAHOMA

Mon. PM

Dear Mom and Pop -

We're all on our toes down her

since yesterday's news of the Jap attack.

Henry Day letter, December 9, 1941. *Collections of the Missouri Historical Society*

"HOW DOES IT FEEL TO BE AT WAR AGAIN?" — LT. HENRY DAY, US ARMY

When the bombs fell at Pearl Harbor, St. Louisan Henry Day was a young Army officer stationed at Fort Sill, Oklahoma. Henry's pursuit of an Army career followed that of his father, Charles, who had fought in France during World War I. In the 1920s, Charles Day and his brother-in-law founded the Valley Dolomite Company. The company processed industrial dolomite for construction and later operated mines in the Mineral Area of Missouri south of St. Louis. The success of the family business allowed the Day family to lead a comfortable life at their home on Clay Avenue in Kirkwood. Henry attended Country Day School before getting accepted to Harvard. It was in October 1941 that he entered the Army and began his training as an officer at the Field Artillery School at Fort Sill.

Just two days after Pearl Harbor, Henry wrote to his parents back in St. Louis and provided them with the situational climate at Fort Sill. Henry's tone seems to express a bit of excitement rather than hesitation, but there is little doubt that those serving knew it was only a matter of time before the inevitable happened and their time to fight would come. Given his father's service in the Great War, Henry was likely eager to do his part to retain the family legacy. His life as an officer was secured and moving forward, and his words expressed delight at the thought of coming home for Christmas.

> Mon. PM
>
> Dear Mom and Pop—
>
> We're all on our toes down here since yesterday's news of the Jap attack. Special guards for fire and sabotage, but otherwise little change. Heard the initial flash about 2 PM yesterday afternoon and sat by the radio most of the night. Also heard the President's speech this AM. Very good. We're very disappointed in the lack of definite news. It's all very much the same—just listened to an announcement in Manila discussing the weather!
>
> How does it feel to be at war again?
>
> I got my leave OK'd Saturday—ten (10) days effective Dec. 24th—and from the latest dope it will not be canceled. At present the policy in the 8th Corp Area is to let all leave and furloughs go thru on schedule. Hope mines does. If so I'll be home in a little over two weeks. I'll be in uniform all the time tho! By the way, I have my new boots, all bought and paid for, so don't worry about them. Have just worn my feet off wearing them. Tomorrow we start on a two-day 50 mile march! I have to get up at 4 AM tomorrow to get off in the advanced detail. We will ride 20-25 miles and set up camp for the rest of the platoon who will follow on foot. Carrying everything on mule packs. Wednesday morning we will come back by a different route and give

a demonstration for the School as we approach camp here. Tomorrow they ride and walk all morning without stopping—except for a 10 min per hr or eating. I'm looking forward to it very much.

Our battalion and regiment have been reorganized and redesignated to cut personal overhead. I am now in Btry 'E', 26th Bn, 6th Eng, Regt.—The 26th is, or was, a horse battalion, now both horse-drawn and mule. The 34th Bn is no more. I am to be appointed administration officer of the Battery. It is not a normal duty of any one person (except of the B.C.), but they are leaving me the job of making up collection sheets and payrolls, etc. Now I'll be mess officer and assistant platoon leader, as well as administration officer—and gas officer (a theoretical job).

More later.

Devotedly,

Henry
Ft. Sill, OK

The letters that Henry wrote home provide a good glimpse of the Army's situation in the days and weeks following the start of the war. One thing was clear: the US was not in a position to immediately fight. Senior leaders in Washington were attempting to come up with the first plans for battlefield preparedness, and the first order of business was acquiring critically needed arms and equipment and attempting to protect American assets that were threatened overseas.

War production began to increase at a continually higher rate starting in 1939 in response to Roosevelt's Protective Mobilization Plan. With the start of World War II in Europe, the Roosevelt administration began to prepare for defensive needs, and the US was woefully behind. At the time, the US military was the ninth largest in the world behind Romania. It was not difficult to understand that America was vulnerable in a world where mechanized armies in Europe and Asia were rolling over smaller, weaker countries.

The point was driven even deeper when Great Britain, a much more defensively prepared nation, was reeling and about to topple under the strain of Germany's industrial-strength forces.

Roosevelt issued production targets that would at least get the country in a better position to defend itself if attacked. In 1940, Roosevelt signed executive orders that called for US aviation companies to build 50,000 aircraft per year, an enormous task considering that all American aircraft manufacturers combined in 1939 completed just over 5,000 aircraft. Tanks were also in critically low numbers. The US tank inventory consisted of around 500 light tanks as compared to German and Japanese tank stocks that numbered in the thousands. The same was true of other essential equipment, such as antiaircraft guns and cannons. There was a lot of catching up to do.

There was also a critical lack of manpower. The Army had 190,000 men in service and 20,000 airmen in the Army Air Corps, which had a fleet of 1,700 mostly outdated and obsolete planes in 1939. The numbers improved slightly over the next two years by introducing the peacetime draft, but recruits were still not in significant numbers to begin an immediate battlefield response when the war began. However, once the Japanese had attacked, enlistment skyrocketed, and the ranks began to fill.

Henry's second letter, written just after the new year, shows that the wheels were starting to turn. The Army was mobilizing, and he noted that companies of men were being shipped elsewhere for assignments, and even some of his fellow officers were beginning to ship out under classified orders. Furthermore, Henry expected to see the arrival of many new young officers at Fort Sill.

> Sunday PM
>
> Dear Mom and Pop—
>
> Not an awful lot of news this time. They've cracked down on us and the coming week should be a busy one with half our (battery) officers on troop convoy duty or leave. But

we won't have many men, most of them leave in the next couple of days, and we haven't gotten in many new ones yet. Several thousand men will be shipped out of here on Tuesday alone! One bunch with secret orders, destination unknown left today with Lt. Eggers (our present battery commander) in charge. Expecting lots of new officers in the next few days. Ross Woolsey of Saint Louis arrived a couple of days ago. He got his Commission at Princeton last June and there's just coming on duty.

The cold snap has finally broken! Instead of near 0 temperatures which predominated last week, yesterday and today have been relatively warm, almost like spring. But I suppose there will be more ice before winter is over.

Henry Day

5 January 1942

As for Henry, his field training continued, but under relatively primitive conditions. The Army's lack of equipment was so poor, Henry explained in his letter, that they were turning to recommissioning and refurbishing museum pieces for the troops to practice with. Military procurement officials were scrambling to find equipment and ammunition to provide for training. They were turning to scouring local armories and other stockpiles to find enough to fill the gap. Many of his training missions still relied heavily on packhorses and mules to transport supplies and provisions. A fully mechanized Army was still months away.

Sunday, Mar 15

Dear Mom and Pop—

By this time I'm well along in school (half-way thru end of this coming week) and have found it simple as falling off a log. Some studying, but largely review. We fired the first time Wednesday and I fired the first problem and hit the target with the first shot! And at a range of 2 ½ miles! We've been firing 4.9 inch guns (model 1905) which were pulled out of museums and renovated recently when large warehouses full of 4.7 in. ammunition were found left over from World War I in the East. There were four of them, but one has broken down completely I think. We're on gunnery now—as you might have guessed—having finished Motors, Materials, and Communication. We fire four days of this week. Dad, you would be interested in the infantry-artillery demonstrations we have Saturday afternoon.

Henry

Luckily for Henry and his comrades, trucks, Jeeps, personnel carriers, and large transport aircraft would replace the horses and mules that he was responsible for coordinating at Fort Sill. A modern mechanized military equal to and later exceeding the other developed nations of the day emerged from the war. It is mind-boggling when one considers that soldiers like Henry were packing mules in 1941, but just four years later, technology had advanced to the point that the American military was training personnel in the ways of radar, jet aircraft, and atomic weapons.

Day's training would take him to North Africa. The Army traded his mules for tanks, and he saw extensive service during the war as a member of the 1st Armored Division Artillery. Henry fought the Germans and Italians in North Africa before crossing the Mediterranean with the invasion of Italy. Upon his return to St. Louis, Henry joined the family business and took over its Bonne Terre, Missouri, operations. He served as the company's president until 1981. He lived to the age of 90 and passed away in 2010.

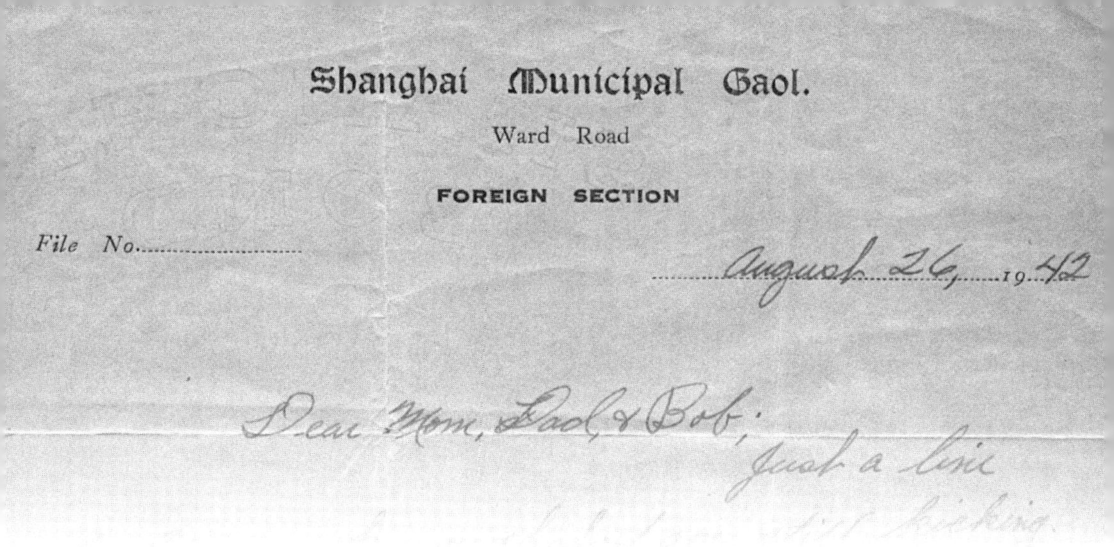
Shanghai Municipal Gaol.
Ward Road
FOREIGN SECTION
File No.
August 26, 1942
Dear Mom, Dad & Bob;
Just a line

PFC Charles Stewart letter, August 26, 1942. *Collections of the Missouri Historical Society*

"GEE IT HAS BEEN A LONG TIME SINCE I HAVE BEEN HOME."

— PFC CHARLES STEWART, US MARINE CORPS

After the Japanese attacks on Pearl Harbor and Manila, American, British, and Dutch diplomats, government officials, and civilian expatriates living in Asian settlements such as Hong Kong, Singapore, and Dutch Indonesia scrambled to evacuate. Many became trapped and were forced into internment camps run by the Japanese military. Here most were held for the duration of the war.

One of the unlucky Americans to be taken prisoner immediately following America's declaration of war on Japan was St. Louisan

Marine Private Charles Stewart, a 20-year-old guard at the US Embassy in Peiping, China. Typically, by agreement and according to the observed international laws of the Geneva Convention, diplomats of all countries are protected from persecution and detention by means of diplomatic immunity. However, Stewart soon discovered that the Japanese would not adhere to protecting US Marine embassy guards like himself because the Japanese recognized them as foreign troops, not diplomats.

On December 7, a detachment of Japanese troops surrounded the US Embassy in Peking, the present city of Beijing. At 1 p.m., according to Stewart's recollections, the Marines surrendered. A similar situation was happening at the American Consulate in the northern Chinese port city of Tientsin. In both cases, officers of the Imperial Japanese army approached the commanding officers of the Marine units and demanded that they put down their weapons and surrender peacefully. In both cases, the commanding officers did so because they believed that the Japanese would honor the Marines' diplomatic immunity and allow everyone to be repatriated. Indeed, the Japanese officers had initially implied that this would be the case. However, a couple of days after the Marines had given themselves over to the Japanese, American officials learned through diplomatic channels that the Japanese government had declared that "it is unable to agree to include United States Marine Guards remaining in China as they constitute a military unit."

At no point were the Marine commanders aware of the diplomatic communications debating their fate. Instead, the Marines were kept in the dark and told by their captors that they were not prisoners of war and repatriation would occur once the details were worked out. Until then, however, the Japanese officers informed them that they would be treated as prisoners and sent to a prison camp for detainment. Weeks went by with no word on their fate.

Then, on February 2, 1942, almost two months after being taken captive, the Marines were sent to the Woosung Prison camp near Shanghai. There they found other Marines who were taken prisoner after the American base on Wake Island was overrun by Japanese troops in an amphibious invasion of the island in late December 1941. Among the prisoners taken there were two other St. Louisans, Private Buell S. Brown and Corporal Henry S. Durrwatcher Jr. Both were lucky to be alive since the fighting on Wake Island had been intense, and following the takeover by the Japanese troops, treatment of the prisoners had been brutal. Many of the prisoners were civilian contractors who had been caught on the island after the conflict began. At one point, the commander in charge of the Japanese forces forced 100 of the civilians down to the beach, where they were lined up and machine-gunned. The officer who gave the order, Rear Admiral Shigematsu Sakaibara, and the officers who complied were later tried at the end of the war for war crimes and hanged.

Soon after Stewart arrived at Woosung came the realization that the captive Marines would remain as prisoners and sent to various camps rather than repatriated as promised. Some of the Marines were sent to prisons in Japan, while others were moved around to other camps in China.

Conditions at the camps were stark and brutal. The men were informed of the prison regulations and told they could be executed for violating rules such as using more than one blanket, talking without permission, or raising their voices. In China, where Stewart was held, the winter of 1942 was a battle of survival against the cold northern China wind. Despite the freezing conditions, they had only what remained of their uniforms for protection. Only the thin blankets they had been provided, and which they wrapped around their shoulders like shawls, kept them from freezing to death.

Neither were the prisoners given adequate food. The Japanese provided them with small rations of rice, fish, and seaweed. Stewart lost 70 pounds over the course of his imprisonment. According to the Geneva Convention, the men were supposed to receive care packages and regular visits from the Red Cross, but this was denied, as well. Stewart would tell American investigators after the war that he never saw a Red Cross representative or received any care packages.

In March 1942, about three months after they had been taken prisoner, Stewart and three other Marines planned their escape. On March 31, the four men managed to free themselves. They headed south and found refuge with a band of Chinese guerrilla fighters, but unfortunately, about 18 days after their escape, Japanese soldiers recaptured them. They were returned to prison and placed in the Bridge House, a notorious Japanese torture center in Shanghai. For 76 days, Stewart was subjected to regular beatings and torture by means of the "water cure," where he was forced to consume large quantities of water for the purpose of causing him severe gastric distress and water intoxication.

When it was over, he was taken to military court and given a sentence of four years in prison for desertion. This resulted in Stewart being transferred to Ward Road jail, considered to be the largest prison in the world at the time; it was also deemed to be escape-proof. Stewart soon proved them wrong.

Stewart and seven other men were in communication with a group of Danish boys who had been freed from the prison. The boys delivered hacksaws to Stewart, and the men sawed their way out of the jail. Once again, they were on the run but captured quickly. Like before, they were sent to the Bridge House and tortured. For the second escape, they were sentenced to death, but the judgment was later rescinded and changed to 14 years in prison.

To serve their terms, Stewart and the other Marines were sent to Nanjing Prison Camp. This proved to be the worst period of imprisonment for them all. There they found themselves kept in one dank, filthy, vermin-filled 9-by-14 cell with no ventilation. The summers were incredibly hot and winters cold. They had no blankets, no beds, no medicine or medical treatment, no heat, and very little food or water. Among Stewart's fellow prisoners in Nanjing was J. B. Powell, an American civilian newspaper reporter who had been arrested by the Japanese when the war began. Powell would lose both his legs to frostbite due to exposure in the prison, a sobering indication of the conditions the men endured.

The Japanese did, however, allow Stewart to write home on occasion. Doing so allowed the Japanese to appear as though they were providing humane treatment. Although the men couldn't say much about the conditions or treatment by their captors, this letter written on Shanghai War-prisoner's Camp stationary on March 26, 1943, almost three years into his imprisonment, provides some insight into his captivity.

> 26th March 1943
>
> Dear Mom, Dad & Bob;
>
> Just a few lines to let you know that I am still kicking, I have received 3 letters from you, and very glad to get them. Please when you write give me all of the family news, and what else you can.
>
> Mother don't send me anything but letters that is all I want, I hope you understand, you have probably heard about me, so I guess you do. Damit that is just it, you know all about me and everything, and I know nothing. I don't know anything about the outside world, except what you tell me in your letters. So when you write inlighten me.
>
> We had a very mild winter the first Christmas I have seen with out snow, It didn't seem like Christmas at all. It must have been 80 Fahrenheit. It snowed here one night, and was all gone by noon the next day. The rest of the winter the weather was just perfect, except a few days.
>
> I am allowed to write a letter every three months, and a card every month. I have received one letter from Aunt Nell, will you please acknowledge it for me.
>
> Please tell every one to write, letters, are like a oasis in a desert.
>
> I am growing my fourth beard, I started this one October 1, 1943, I think I will keep it.

Have you received any letters from me?

I have to close now, all my love.

Your son,

Charles A. Stewart, Jr.

His plea to his mother not to send anything but letters was likely an indication that he knew that it would be a waste of her time to do so. There was little chance that he would receive anything she might have sent. Stewart would later state that he received only a handful of letters from home, and in turn his family received only a few from him despite him writing and sending about 25 over the course of his detainment.

As Stewart stated in his letter, he and his fellow Marines knew little of what was happening in the outside world. It came then as a surprise on August 15, 1945, when the officer of the day had their cells opened and told them to assemble before the prison's commanding officer. He addressed the men by saying, "You are now being released by the kindness and courtesy of the Japanese people. The war is over. We are so sorry for your treatment but due to the outstanding differences of our two countries we could not give you the treatment accorded to prisoners of the Americans."

The officer failed to mention Japan's surrender. Stewart said the commander asked for a salute, and as he bowed low, the prisoners thumbed their noses at him. From Nanjing, they were taken to an American refugee camp. He came home to St. Louis shortly thereafter.

Wartime changes all men, but the experiences of those held as POWs add another layer of tragedy to the already difficult circumstances of combat. Upon his return, Stewart spent time with his family and convalesced. In April 1946, he married Dolores Peterson and began a new life. He died in Houston, Texas, at the age of 56 in 1978. Charles A. Stewart Jr. is buried in Forest Park Westheimer Cemetery in Houston, Texas.

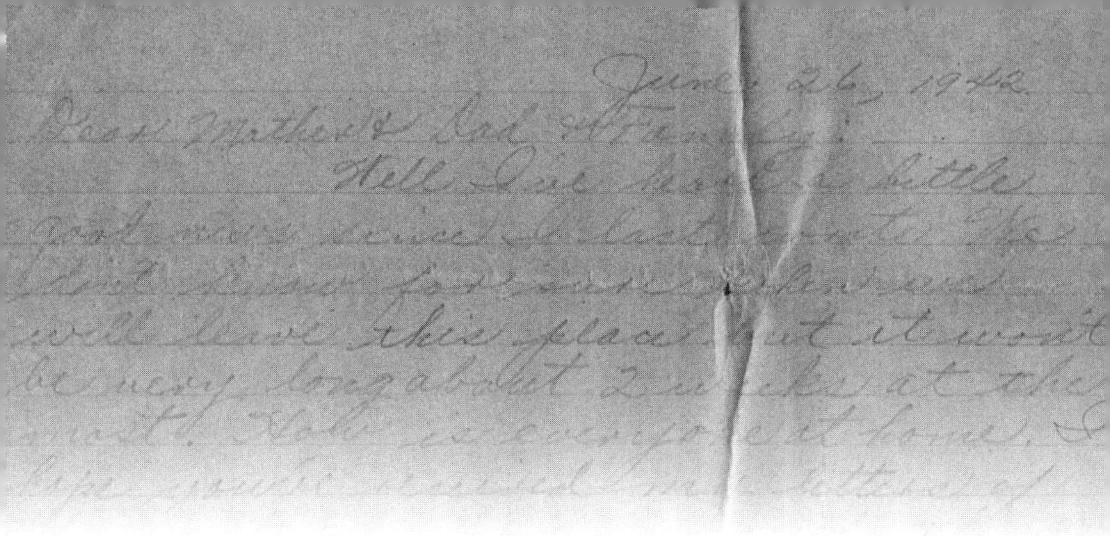
June 26, 1942
Dear Mother & Dad & Family:
Well I've had a little

Lawrence Kennedy letter, June 26, 1942. *Collections of the Missouri Historical Society*

"I'M SAFE & SOUND." — LAWRENCE KENNEDY, US MERCHANT MARINE

The first year of the war was marked by painful losses on the war front and major adjustments on the home front. As the first months of 1942 progressed, Japan and Germany had the upper hand, and this extended to combat at sea. On the Atlantic, German U-boats were causing catastrophic disruption of supply convoys to Britain. In the first six months of 1942, the US had lost almost 400 ships to U-boats along the Eastern Seaboard and the Gulf of Mexico. The frequency of attacks off the North Carolina coast earned it the name "Torpedo Junction," as 90 ships were sunk in these waters alone. Crossings were dangerous undertakings, but convoys of supplies and men had to get through.

If the US and Great Britain were to defeat the Nazis, they would need a constant line of men, equipment, and supplies flowing across the Atlantic to the British Isles. Millions of tons of cargo was the fuel that powered the war machine, and it all had to be shipped on merchant vessels sailing from ports like New York, Baltimore, New Orleans, and Houston. A fleet of vessels dedicated to this task, designated as Liberty Ships, began production in 1941, and the first of its kind, *Patrick Henry*, slid down the launch at the Bethlehem Sparrows Point Shipyard in Baltimore in 1942. It took 244 days to build.

These workhorses of the merchant fleet were built at 18 dockyards on the East and West Coasts. When production ended in 1945, more than 2,700 had been built. The men responsible for manning these vessels were members of the US Merchant Marine. These sailors performed their duties under extremely dangerous conditions, as convoys of merchant ships were under constant threat of attack by German U-boats in the Atlantic and Gulf of Mexico. Unlike naval ships, these ships were largely unarmed and had to rely on safety in numbers to make successful passage. Large convoys of hundreds of ships made the trek across the Atlantic escorted by the Navy, but attacks by groups of stealthy U-boats, known as wolf packs, took a tremendous toll.

More than 250,000 men would serve as Merchant Mariners during the war. Among that number was a young man from St. Louis named Lawrence Kennedy. The Kennedys were a big family. Lawrence was the third oldest of eight and was working for a dairy before he decided to join up as a Mariner. Service to their country seemed to come naturally to the Kennedy boys. Lawrence's oldest brother, Carl, enlisted in the Army Air Corps but later did his service with the 138th Engineers in New Guinea and the Philippines. Thomas joined the Navy, as did Robert, Lawrence's younger brother. Robert served in an amphibious landing craft unit and saw duty aboard *LST-117* and *LST-969* in the South Pacific. The last brother, Theodore, served in the Signal Corps and was shipped to England to serve with a B-17 unit, the 398th Bombardment Group of the Eighth Air Force.

The Kennedy brothers must have had the luck of the Irish on their side because all of them returned home safely. This blessing was definitely present in Lawrence, who had the good fortune of surviving not one but two close calls during his time sailing aboard the Liberty Ships and merchant vessels. Reading Lawrence's letter written to his family after his rescue, one gets the impression that he saw the risks and the situations that befell him as simply occupational hazards. Perhaps taking it lightly was the way to keep from giving in to the anxieties of everyday life on the seas while being hunted by submarines. Yet, he saw his comrades die and experienced the grave dangers of the life of merchant sailors. His letter reassures his mother that he had healed from his "fish bites," which hardly gives an accurate description of his encounter.

When Lawrence signed up for the Merchant Marine, he wasn't alone. Three of his buddies joined with him: James Thompson, Robert Frank McGee, and Stanley Gibson. The men were sent to St. Petersburg, Florida, for training at the U.S. Maritime Service Training Station, where they completed their sailor fitness before leaving for New Orleans. In the Crescent City, they joined the crew of the SS *Hermis*, a Panamanian-registered steamship that made regular trips between New Orleans and Aruba. The ship was new to the US merchant fleet. It had been operated by an Italian shipping company but was seized by the US government only one month prior to the start of the war and transferred to the Lykes Brothers Steamship Company, which was under contract with the War Department. The boat's master was a seasoned sailor, Master Thomas Stanborough, an Australian-born resident of New Orleans.

In May 1942, the *Hermis* got underway for its run to Aruba. The ship's route was to take it to several ports to load and off-load cargo: first to Tampa, Florida, then on to Panama before heading to Venezuela and finally the island of Aruba. The back-and-forth course made the ship vulnerable, and there was no escort. The *Hermis* was unarmed and alone. Hundreds of merchant ships had been torpedoed in the first few months of 1942, and the Caribbean was a hunting ground for U-boats seeking to increase their kill ratios and cripple Allied supply chains.

On June 7, the *Hermis* was about 50 miles off the western tip of Cuba when it was spotted by U-boat Captain Erwin Rostin, commander of *U-158*. Rostin was a fairly new member of the U-boat service. He had previously commanded minesweepers before transferring to the U-boat command in early 1941. In September 1941, Rostin was commissioned command of the *U-158*, a large well-armed submarine that could carry up to 22 torpedoes and 66 mines in addition to its deck gun. After Germany declared war on the US in December, Rostin took *U-158* to the rich hunting grounds off the coastal United States, where he sunk five ships on his first patrol, sending 38,000 tons of cargo to the bottom of the Atlantic before returning home to Germany.

In May 1942, Rostin left for his second patrol. It would prove to be even more fruitful than the first. Rather than returning to the East Coast, *U-158* patrolled the Gulf of Mexico. Throughout May and June, 12 more boats fell victim to Rostin's torpedoes, including the *Hermis*.

On that day, Lawrence Kennedy and his mates were on deck when the ship's port side was struck by Rostin's first shot from *U-158*. Kennedy later told a reporter, "The force of the impact knocked me and a lot of fellows into the water." The damage was just ahead of the ship's bridge, and now a direct hit on the port side sent the boat shuddering and spinning. The *Hermis*, however, did not come to a stop; a broken deck valve kept the engines from stopping, and it continued to circle in the waves at about eight knots. Rostin was determined to destroy the vessel and surfaced. The submarine's deck guns opened fire and struck the wheelhouse and chart room, setting the ship on fire. This was apparently sufficient for Rostin, and he left the *Hermis* to flounder. It would take about 12 hours for the boat to slip beneath the waterline.

Meanwhile, Lawrence was in the water as the chaos ensued. At the time, he did not know that his friend Stanley Gibson had been taking a shower at the time of impact. Feeling the impact and likely fearful that he might get caught within the damaged ship, Stanley did not wait to dress but grabbed a survival vest and headed to the deck to safety. The naked seaman leapt into the sea. It was there that Stanley encountered yet more danger. For as the men thrashed about in the open water, they attracted the attention of hungry sharks. As he floated, Stanley was attacked and killed.

Lawrence did not mention it to the news reporter, but as his letter states, he too suffered shark bites, apparently as he and 16 other crew members clung to an overturned lifeboat. It was afterward that he learned of his friend Stanley's fate. He told the reporter that Stanley's situation may have come about due to his lack of clothing and that the Merchant Marine taught sailors that they should always wear trousers while in the water since sharks will be attracted to white skin before dark clothing.

A US Coast Guard patrol plane spotted the stranded seamen, and 45 of the 47 crewmen of the *Hermis* made it to safety. Only Stanley and another were lost. Lawrence was taken to Jamaica to rest and recover. It is from here that he wrote this letter letting his family know that he was safe and awaiting new orders.

> June 26, 1942
>
> Dear Mother, Dad, and Family
>
> Well I've had a little good news since I last wrote. We don't know for sure when we will leave this place but it won't be very long about 2 weeks at the most. How is everyone at home. I hope you'ved received my letters of the past and have answered them. My address is the same
>
> Mr. Lawrence Kennedy
> 41 South Camp Road
> Kingston Jamaica
> B.W.I.
>
> Be sure and write Special Delivery Air Mail as it will be impossible for me to get the letters. You see air mail is the

only safe way mail can arrive here. There's nothing new here. I've been going on picnics and swimming and to the movies. All the movies are about a year old but a fellow has to go somewhere to pass the time away and that is where I go to get my sleep. It is the only cool place in town.

Last week I went to a dance given by the English Consol. It was a nice dance and all but I can't get used to these English customs. They serve tea and crumpets (crackers with cheese) for lunch. I sure as the devil can'ts live on tea and crackers and the rest of the meals aren't bad but you just about starve to death getting use to them. You see Jamaica is an island and depends mostly on shipping for its foodstuffs. All its meals are imported. At the present time they can't get fresh meats & they serve us goat meat. After you get used to it and make up your mind that it's all you can have it's all right but that getting used to it just about killed me. I saw another show last night and today I'll read a magazine or a book. The lady of the house is very nice to us & does everything she can for us but it still isn't home that's where I'm headed if I can get off the island. You see I lost all my identification papers Fireman papers & birth certificate when the ship went down.

I also lost all my clothes. Everything is being taken care of & I've been given clothes and all my papers will be reissued to me. This takes time. The company is paying all our expenses and giving us spending money which will be taken out of our salary later. I'm safe & sound and the few fish bites I had on my arm are healed up. They took the bandages off yesterday. I hope everyone is well at home.

I also lost that address book with everything else or I would write the Aunts & Uncles. Tell them all hello when you see them. Mother don't go working too hard around the house and tell Pop hello. How are all the kids?

Write soon

Your loving son

Lawrence

The sinking of the *Hermis* was a harrowing experience, but Lawrence's service continued, and after his respite in Jamaica, he was aboard another vessel. In May 1943, Lawrence's ship would suffer the same consequences as the *Hermis*, though the circumstances were not as dire. This time, he and his crewmates were rescued and taken to Belize. Lawrence served on three more Liberty Ships during the remainder of the war.

There was also justice for Stanley and the *Hermis*. On June 30, 1942, 24 days after the sinking of Lawrence's ship, Erwin Roskin surfaced in the Atlantic near Bermuda to radio to German Naval Intelligence the contents of important documents his crew had captured from a ship. The lengthy open communications allowed US Navy radio monitors to pinpoint the location of the sub. A Navy anti-sub plane was dispatched, and it approached the *U-158* undetected by flying in low cloud cover. Rostin was taken by surprise as the Flying Boat dove out of the sun and dropped two depth charges immediately next to the submarine. They detonated directly under *U-158*'s stern, sinking her immediately and taking all 54 crewmen with her.

THEIR SONS WERE KILLED IN ACTION

—U. S. Coast Guard Photo

Lieut. Commander O. C. D. Wev, (extreme left), director of the United States Coast Guard Reserve for St. Louis, is shown yesterday awarding National Maritime Union medals to two mothers whose sons were killed in action and to sailors who were recently on ships torpedoed by Axis submarines in the Caribbean. In the front are Mrs. Opal Knies (left) of Peoria, whose son, Robert, perished, and Mrs. Tillie Gibson of 1921A North Thirteenth street, whose son, Stanley, was a victim of Axis undersea warfare. In the back are, from the left: Lawrence Kennedy, 2938 North Euclid avenue; Pete Frisella, 4959 Emerson avenue; Dean Edwards of Hettick, Ill., and James Thompson, 6209 Lorraine avenue.

Lawrence Kennedy, pictured back right, was a friend and shipmate of Stanley Gibson, who was killed by a shark attack when their ship was sunk by a German U-boat in the Gulf of Mexico. Stanley's mother received a Merchant Marine medal for his service. *Newspapers.com*

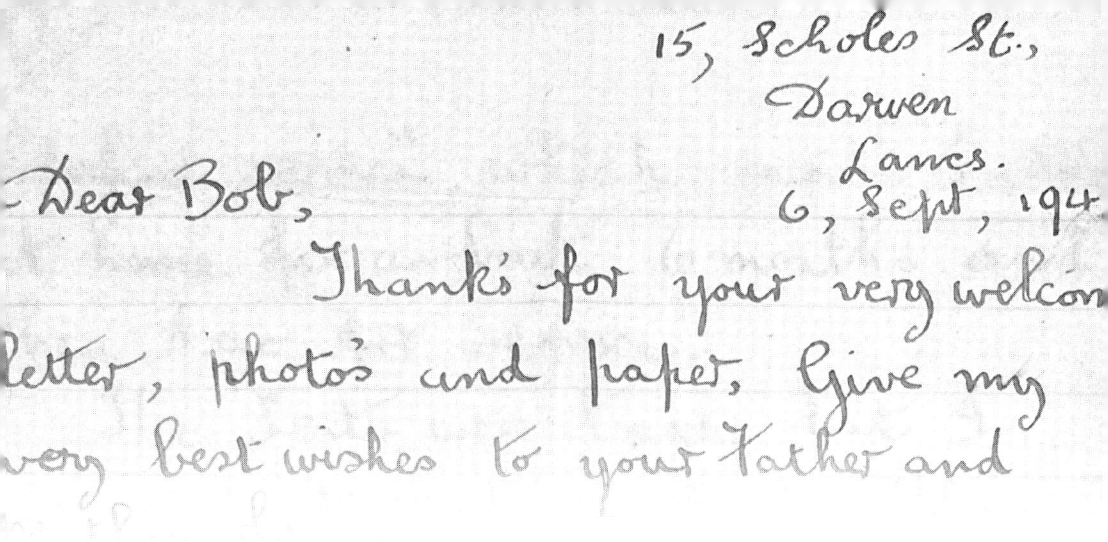

15, Scholes St.,
Darwen
Lancs.
6, Sept, 194
Dear Bob,
Thank's for your very welcom
letter, photo's and paper, Give my
very best wishes to your Father and

Fred RAF letter, September 6, 1942. *Collections of the Missouri Historical Society*

"TELL EVERYONE OVER THERE TO KEEP THERE [SIC] CHINS UP."

— FRED, ROYAL AIR FORCE, TO ST. LOUIS PEN PAL, ROBERT SHIELDS

Americans who watched the newsreels shown at their local theaters and read the newspapers were keenly aware of Great Britain's bitter struggle to remain as the last holdout against Hitler's plan for total European domination. A year before Pearl Harbor, Americans watched as Hitler's Luftwaffe pummeled London and other major cities in the UK with daily bombings that killed more than 23,000 innocent civilians and reduced miles of homes, businesses, and factories to rubble in just under four months. The Battle of Britain, also known as the Blitz, stunned Americans with its blatant disregard for the lives of innocent civilians, particularly women and children. It was clear to see that Britain, America's closest ally, was hanging on by its fingertips, yet with dogged determination, it remained united and strong and showed Hitler that he would not wear them down.

The first line of defense against the German air force was Britain's Royal Air Force. The bravery and sacrifice demonstrated by the RAF during the Battle of Britain won over the hearts of Americans who viewed His Majesty's pilots as nothing less than heroes. When America entered the war against Germany just four days after the Japanese attack on Pearl Harbor, the British no doubt breathed a sigh of relief that help was on the way, but Americans also were comforted to know that Britain's RAF would be fighting alongside American flyers to bring down Hitler's Messerschmitt fighters and Junkers bombers.

One of the technical advantages held by the RAF was their use of the Spitfire fighter. It was a superbly designed, powerful fighter that easily matched, and could outmaneuver, the Germans' formidable Messerschmitt 109 fighter. The Spitfires and their pilots were champions of the sky, a fact that was not lost on young Bob Shields of St. Louis. In 1942, 15-year-old Bob saw a notice in a comic book encouraging kids to become pen pals. When he responded to the ad, he was paired with Fred, a Royal Air Force recruit, in Darwen, Lancashire, England. Unfortunately, the letter contained no last name, so Fred's full identity is not known.

Fred's town of Darwen lies north of Manchester in north central England. During the Battle of Britain in the late summer of 1940, smaller towns were mostly spared from the terrifying carnage of the Luftwaffe's aerial bombing, but Darwen had the misfortune of twice being a target of the German air raids. On October 21, 1940, near the end of the Blitz, German Junkers rained bombs on the town, killing six during the first raid. A couple of days later the planes returned, causing more casualties, including machine-gunning a civilian bus traveling along a country road. The Luftwaffe's actions demonstrated that Hitler and his air marshals were not just focused on big cities like London and other industrial centers.

Fred responded to Bob's pen pal letter in September 1942. The letter is a perfect slice of the youth culture of the day and speaks of learning to play the drums, swing music, and movie magazines. Despite Fred's promise to write again, apparently no other letters were received. We can only hope that Fred simply failed to write.

> 15, Scholes St,
> Darwen, Lancs.
>
> 6, Sept, 1942
>
> Dear Bob,
>
> Thanks for your very welcome letter, photo's and paper, give my best wishes to your father and mother for me.
>
> Glad to hear about your musical abilities, personally, I play the drums (real swing style) and a friend of mine, Miss Irene Tattelsall sings the vocal numbers with a local band called the "Mayfair Accordion Band"
>
> If you have any catalogue's for drum kits, I should like to have a look at them.
>
> Here's a bit a news that will surprise you. I volunteered for flying duties with the RAF and went away for three days to take my exams. I passed O.K. and I am now on "deferred service" which means I stay at home for about 6 months and then I go for service.
>
> The tests were tough but I managed it, and am I glad (Whoopee!!).
>
> Well, the A.T.C went to camp and had we a good time. We were at a seaside resort and every night we went making merry on all the amusements.
>
> We also had flights in RAF planes.

Your letter arrived with one from Smitty and I shall send papers and photo's as soon as I can. I am sending you a ATC magazine along with the letter, let me know if you get it O.K. and if you like it.

By the way I have been promoted to corporal.

Tell everyone over there to keep there [sic] chins up, this war is tougher on the enemy then with us, and we have the advantage of knowing we fight for the right.

Don't forget to write a quick reply and I like Movie Magazines!!

Cheerio for now

Fred

P.S. Please write your address in letter.

RAF

"Through Hell to Heaven"

When Bob Shields himself became old enough to enlist, he joined the Army in November 1945. We don't know what became of Fred and his RAF career. What is known is that a stainless steel sculpture of an RAF Spitfire now stands in the town center of Darwen. It commemorates the *Borough of Darwen*, an RAF Spitfire purchased with money raised by the townspeople of Darwen following the Blitz. The *Borough of Darwen* fighter went into service in the spring of 1941 but was sadly lost later that summer over France while escorting bombers.

The sleek sculpture erected in Darwen's Town Centre in 2012 represents not only the superior aerodynamics that helped protect Britain from the might of the German war machine but also the ability of the British people to stay strong in the face of adversity and contribute to the war effort with whatever they could sacrifice.

Bob Shields never forgot Fred's letter and kept it all his life. Bob passed away in 2008 and rests in Jefferson Barracks National Cemetery.

During the Battle of Britain in 1940, Royal Air Force Spitfire fighters were capable of outmaneuvering the German Luftwaffe's Messerschmitt 109s. *National Archives*

"EVERY ST. LOUIS HOME MUST GET IN THE SCRAP."

This statement concluded an editorial in the *Globe-Democrat* regarding the need to donate any scrap metal toward the war effort. Nearly all new steel production was going directly toward the wartime production of planes, equipment, guns, and ammunition, but it still was not enough to keep production targets on track. The *Globe* article, which announced that the newspaper was leading the local scrap metal drive initiative in St. Louis in the fall of 1942, stated that 17 million tons of additional metal was needed to keep America's steel plants operating at full capacity.

The whole region responded enthusiastically, and drives were launched by Boy Scouts, churches, clubs, and other community groups. Everyone was urged to scour their attics, basements, and barns for anything metal they could spare. The Army sent convoys of trucks along with cranes and loaders to pick up tons of scrap across the region. Units from Fort Leonard Wood collected buckets, old machinery, old bed springs, washtubs, nails, wire fencing, sheet metal, and anything else they could melt down. From St. Louis to Farmington, Bonne Terre, and Hillsboro, a string of 25 Army trucks loaded whatever they could collect in one drive in 1943.

But it wasn't just metal that was needed. When the US went to war with Japan, the country lost its access to vital rubber supplies that were primarily extracted from rubber plantations in places like Indonesia, now occupied by the Empire of the Sun. In June 1942, President Roosevelt took to the radio to ask Americans to find and donate whatever rubber they could spare. St. Louis was expected to contribute at least 2 million pounds to the effort. When the city fell behind in its quota, the newspapers chided the public for not doing more. They employed civic competition to try to push more people to step forward with old garden hoses and such by noting that Kansas City had a smaller population but had already donated more than St. Louis. Belleville and East St. Louis had met their expectations too.

The metal and rubber built the items needed to win the war. One of the exciting ways to get communities involved was the Buy a Bomber campaign. This program allowed communities to raise funds by buying war bonds that would be put toward funding the completion of a Flying Fortress. The bomber could be named after the community that purchased it. The American Legion Auxiliary of Missouri had the distinction of being the first Legion Auxiliary in the US to meet the purchasing requirement. Many of the organizations that jumped on the Buy a Bomber bandwagon were women's clubs such as the Women's International Bowling Congress and the Missouri Federation of Women's Clubs. The Buy a Bomber campaign became extremely popular, and communities around the St. Louis region were proud to sponsor B-17s sporting names like the *Spirit of Crawford County* and the *Spirit of St. Francois*. In St. Louis, the students of the St. Louis Public Schools purchased

The students of St. Louis Public Schools participated in the War Department's Buy a Bomber program by buying enough bonds to purchase two P-51 Mustangs, including the *Stinger* pictured here and the *St. Louis Tornado* B-17 Flying Fortress bomber. *Collections of the Missouri Historical Society*

three planes, a Flying Fortress named the *St. Louis Tornado* and two P-51 pursuit planes named the *Gremlin* and the *Stinger*.

When rationing was put into place to conserve items needed for the war effort, food was naturally one of the items to be rationed. Just as in World War I, people turned to home gardening to supplement what they could purchase at the grocery store. Many older people remembered planting victory gardens during the Great War. Now it was time to roll up their sleeves and get their hands in the soil once again.

The Victory Garden Movement was a project of the Home Food Supply Program, a nationwide cooperative effort in 30 states. In Missouri, the garden movement was successful but less so in urban areas. St. Louis victory garden proponents encouraged city dwellers to plant garden plots in backyards and lots. Many communities encouraged gardens by offering yearly competitions for the best gardens or produce. The Missouri Botanical Garden hosted a Victory Garden Harvest Show in late 1942 to do its part to promote the movement.

The Missouri Farm Bureau and the St. Louis County University Extension offered workshops for new gardeners and other guidance for those who dug into the idea. Like contemporary movements promoting gardening as a form of mindfulness with mental health

Civil Defense Warden Herman Graf proudly displays his insignias and victory garden. *Collections of the Missouri Historical Society*

benefits, a St. Louis Health official told the *Globe-Democrat* in 1943 that having a victory garden did more than produce food. Gardeners would reap the benefits of "exercise, make good use of leisure time, and have the benefit of fine mental relaxation in a time of mental trial."

Besides food, tires and gasoline were the most important items to be affected by war rationing. St. Louisans had to get used to driving on retreaded tires for their cars. Gasoline was also rationed. Everyone was urged to drive less and rely on other forms of transportation. In 1942, when rationing was introduced, many began to speculate that the day of the horse and buggy had returned.

St. Louis's only remaining livery stable owner soon reported that he was receiving calls from those inquiring about services. Earl Weule operated a stable and blacksmith shop interestingly enough on the site where Wells Fargo Express Company had its St. Louis headquarters in the days before the automobile. "I'm convinced," he said, "that the horse is coming back into its own at a gallop." A couple of local companies even ordered wagons to replace delivery vans. One of those companies was H&S Book Binding Company on Washington Avenue, which sought to replace one of its trucks with a wagon. "We think it's the right thing to do," stated owner C. Don Donnelly. "The horse and wagon have been ordered."

Of course, the trend to replace cars with horses did not take off. People made the best of what they had for family vehicles even if it meant riding on bald tires. Gasoline rationing was introduced in late 1942, first on the East Coast. The system for rationing gas was broken down by users. A private individual whose car had a current registration received an A ration coupon book consisting of six pages with eight coupons on each page. Each coupon was worth four gallons of gas. It was good for two months. If you used all your coupons prior to the two months, you had to wait until the period was over to obtain new coupons. The gas stamps were hot commodities, and soon ration offices across the East were hit with burglaries. In St. Louis, the municipal courts soon found themselves dealing with cases of motorists buying illegal stamp books. The punishment was often confiscating the books and a fine. Ration books could also be taken away for speeding offenses.

The war brought a host of challenges to St. Louis, but those challenges were met with resourcefulness and enthusiasm by the people of the region. Successful war bond drives raised millions for the war effort and allowed people to genuinely contribute to winning the war even though they were at home and not on the battlefield. Victory gardens and surplus drives kept communities involved and helped boost morale because they could see that their contributions were assisting those who were on the front lines.

Otto Rost was the head football and basketball coach for the McKinley High School Goldbugs in the late 1930s and early 1940s. He maintained correspondence with several of his former players throughout the war. Future Ensign J. J. Cook is also in this photo but unfortunately not identified. *Collections of the Missouri Historical Society*

LETTERS TO COACH ROST

A good coach doesn't just lead; he inspires, instills confidence, and mentors, even after the players have left the field. McKinley High School physical education teacher Otto Rost was that caliber of coach. After he finished his own stellar football career playing for the University of Kansas in the early 1930s, Rost returned to St. Louis and began his teaching career with the St. Louis Public Schools.

As head coach for both the basketball and football McKinley High School Goldbugs, Coach Rost led his teams to many victories and was cheered by fans for using brains as well as skill to win games. In 1935, he captured the respect of St. Louis football fans by showing that he would go all in during one of the season's most challenging games. Three years later, *St. Louis Globe-Democrat* sports columnist Maurice O. Shelvin wrote, "The way Rost outsmarted Beaumont in that title game in 1935 is still spoken of in Public High circles."

On that November Saturday in 1935, the players arrived to find the field at Public School Stadium completely frozen solid and iced over. When the teams took the field, neither side could get their footing with their customary football shoes, which didn't provide much grip on the icy ground. Rost sized up the situation and sent a team manager to a neighborhood shoe store with the order to buy the team tennis shoes. The plan worked, and while Beaumont's players continued to slip and slide, McKinley charged ahead to victory.

Like any good leader, he earned and received the loyalty of his followers. His players looked to him for guidance, and he looked to them to give their best on the court and on the gridiron.

After the bombs fell on Pearl Harbor, McKinley graduates and former players found themselves involved in a much more serious competition: a struggle for survival and a race toward victory against much more sinister opponents. Coach Rost's players entered all branches of the service and fought on land and sea. Yet even after the former Goldbugs answered their country's call to duty, keeping in touch with Coach Rost was important. The archives of Jefferson Barracks Park contain a cache of letters written to Rost by his former players from the distant theaters of war. It is possible to feel their admiration through the lines they wrote, and though we do not see Coach Rost's written replies, we know from their responses that he kept the lines of correspondence going. It surely meant a lot to these young men.

USYP-105
% Fleet Postmaster
Norfolk,Va.
March 22, 1943

Dear Otto:
Your letter was indeed a very pleasant surprise, I thought you may have forgotten to answer. You mentioned something about Joe Cook, the odd part about it is that he is right across the base from me and I didn't know it. I am working out of the Section Base at Little Creek Va.and the base Joe is working out of is the very same one,only right across the bay. My headquarters are N.O.B.,Norfolk, but we have to come down to Little Creek to refuel and get our stores. Joe is really in some rugged duty, I don't know whether he has told you about it or not. It is the toughest duty the Navy can give one. That and the Armed guard branch. The Armed guard stuff is where they put you on a Merchant ship and you have charge of a gun crew. I don't like to say this but the boys call it the suicide branch. It is strictly convoy duty.
Our duty is patrolling the Cheaspeake Bay, particu-larly, the Naval Operations Base. We chase all ships that don't

Anthony F. J. Defilio letter, March 22, 1943. *Jefferson Barracks Park*

"GAD, WHAT A DRUNK I AM GOING TO INSTITUTE." — ENSIGN ANTHONY F. J. DEFILIO, US NAVY

Among the letters received by Coach Rost were two written by his former students, Anthony F. J. Defilio and Joe J. Cook. Both were McKinley athletes and, judging from the familiarity with which they addressed Rost, it is clear that they knew him well and considered him a mentor and friend.

Perhaps owing to Rost's influence, Defilio entered college after graduating from McKinley and received a teaching degree in physical education. Before the war, Defilio worked for the WPA Educational Division, a branch of President Franklin D. Roosevelt's Works Progress Administration jobs program that provided opportunities for unemployed teachers. In 1942, Defilio joined the Navy and was stationed at Naval Observation Base Norfolk. His letter, dated 1943, describes his duties and expresses his desire to continue his naval training and join the ranks of those hunting submarines on the high seas.

As an ensign, he was assigned to anti-sub patrol boats in Chesapeake Bay. Censorship prohibited Ensign Defilio from providing details of his experiences while on duty. Yet, he alluded to encounters with U-boats during his time on patrol. These experiences may account for his hopes of joining the larger anti-submarine fleet.

The Chesapeake Bay, Virginia, and Carolina coasts were prime targets for the German subs patrolling the seas for Navy and merchant ships. Before Defilio's service at NOB Norfolk, the German submarine service carried out its most successful attack on US shipping, when on June 12, 1942, *U-701* quietly strung 15 mines in 36 feet of water at the mouth of the Chesapeake. Within hours, two merchant ships were sent to the bottom by the mines, and another three boats were damaged.

U-701 continued to disrupt shipping along the Carolina coast for another three weeks by successfully damaging three more ships with torpedoes and sinking a US Navy patrol boat with its deck gun. Finally, on July 7, an Army Air Corps Hudson light bomber spotted the *U-701* surfacing near Cape Hatteras and went in for the kill. It dropped depth charges that damaged the German submarine enough to sink it.

The Navy's close U-boat encounters in the Chesapeake strengthened its resolve to protect the bay. Defilio's patrol duties illustrate those actions.

Ensign Defilio's letter of March 1943 told Coach Rost how much he looked forward to the end of the war, and of his plans to celebrate once victory was announced. It was a sentiment shared by many of his peers.

USYP-105
c/o Fleet Postmaster

Norfolk, VA
March 22, 1943

Dear Otto:

Your letter was indeed a very pleasant surprise, I thought you may have forgotten to answer. You mentioned something about Joe Cook, the hard part about it is that he is right across the base from me and I didn't know it. I'm working out of the section base at little Creek VA and the base Joe is working out of is the very same one, only right across the Bay. My headquarters are NOB, Norfolk, but we have come down to little creek to refuel and get our stores. Joe is really in some rugged duty, I don't know whether he has told you about it or not. It is the toughest duty the Navy can give one. That and the armed guard branch. The armed guard stuff is where they put you on a merchant ship and you have charge of a gun crew. I don't like to say this but the boys call it the suicide branch. It is strictly convoy duty.

Our duty is patrolling the Chesapeake Bay, particularly, the naval operations base. We chase all ships that don't identify themselves. We have already had some fun with Subs. It was quite an experience, or I should have say experiences. But those were the only times we have seen any real action. Joe will get in some good stuff when they go across, and you can bet your boots it will be hot and heavy constantly

My immediate goal is to become the skipper of one of these patrol boats, and then be sent to PC school down in Miami Beach. From there I will have one of the newer boats and be sent in convoy escort duty. Joe's duty is somewhat similar only he will be bringing men right up on the beaches. I really like this duty, it is chiefly sub chasing and fighting work. At the present time I am the executive officer of this craft, as you will probably notice I am on a different boat. I was transferred right after I sent you my first letter. It is an awfully big break and gives me chance to get to the spot I spoke of. How is your wife and children, you hardly mentioned them in your letter. Tell your wife for me that your best bet is right where you are now, you aren't missing anything out there. I believe I am speaking for all the boys when I say we are all waiting for one only one thing, the day this is over. Gad, what a drunk I am going to institute it is going to be a national obligation for me to remember to get stinko on that day. Thanks for your very nice words of encouragement, and your willingness to help me when we come home. That alone is something to feel very good about. Let me know how you are making out with your teams, I'm very much interested. So long and right when you can period give my best to everyone at home.

Sincerely,

Tony

Anthony Defilio did not remain on the East Coast. By 1944, he was stationed in California, was promoted to lieutenant commander, and was an executive officer commanding a naval storage ship.

When the war did come to an end, Anthony Defilio returned to St. Louis. The St. Louis Public Schools hired him as an assistant physical education teacher, and he coached at Soldan and Central High Schools. He led a distinguished career as a coach and principal as well as becoming a well-known figure in local league sports as an umpire for St. Louis–area baseball games. In 1990, Defilio was inducted into the Greater St. Louis Amateur Baseball Hall of Fame for his years of contributing to the game.

Defilio's career in the Navy did not end once peace was declared. He continued his service in the Naval Reserve until 1973. His devotion to the Navy extended into his education career, as he was responsible for establishing the Sea Cadets program in St. Louis while serving as chairman of the Navy League in the early 1960s. The Sea Cadets, a Navy-affiliated high school ROTC program, prepared high school and middle school students for service in the US Navy.

Captain Anthony F. Defilio, US Navy, passed away in 2000. He rests in Jefferson Barracks National Cemetery.

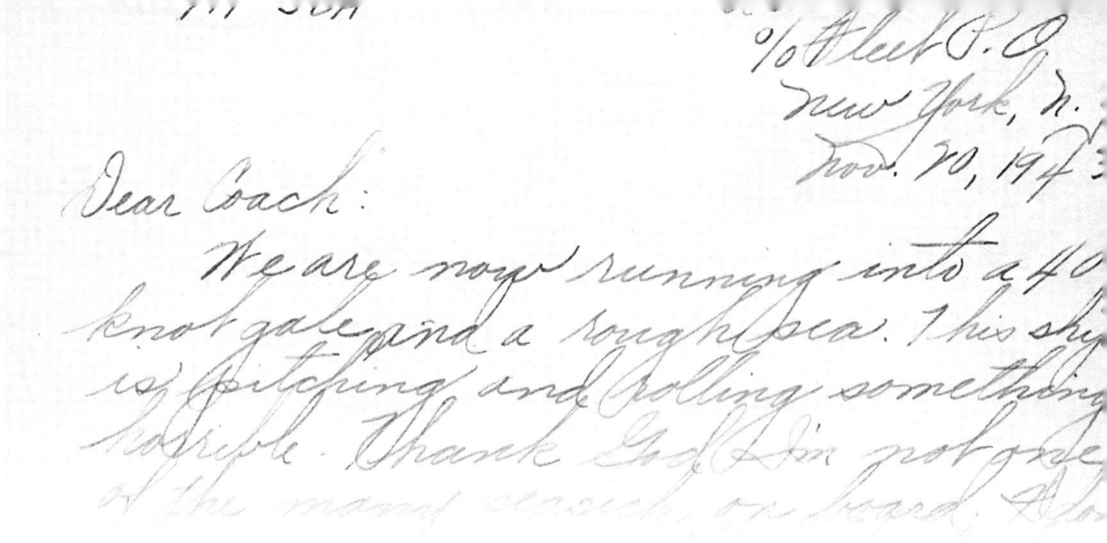
c/o Fleet P.O.
New York, N.
Nov. 10, 194

Dear Coach:

We are now running into a 40 knot gale and a rough sea. This ship is pitching and rolling something horrible. Thank God I'm not one of the many seasick on board.

J. J. Cook letter, November 10, 1943. *Jefferson Barracks Park*

"I REALLY THINK THERE'S [SIC] ISN'T A MORE BEAUTIFUL SIGHT ON WATER THAN THE APPROACH TO NAPLES HARBOR."

— ENSIGN JOSEPH J. COOK, US NAVY

One of the most insightful letters of this period was written by Otto Rost's former student Ensign J. J. Cook aboard the USS *James O'Hara*. Cook's ship was a Frederick Funston-class attack transport assigned to the Mediterranean. In the July and

Cook served aboard the transport ship USS *James O'Hara*, which ferried troops from North Africa to Italy during the Italian campaigns. *National Archives*

September 1943 invasions of Italy, the *O'Hara* hauled American soldiers across the Mediterranean from North Africa to Sicily.

Ensign Cook's letter is one of the more detailed and interestingly uncensored accounts of the life of a World War II serviceman. He touched on topics that allow us to see life as it was for a sailor, sometimes lighthearted and sometimes sobering. As a crewman aboard an attack transport, Cook participated in landing soldiers in the first invasions of Italy and witnessed the destruction carried out by both the US and German forces as the Americans sought to liberate Italy from the fascists and the Germans sought to defend and hold it. But even as he witnessed the devastation, he saw the beauty that remained.

Naples was, to Cook's surprise, a modern city. He likely expected to see an ancient city of Roman and Renaissance buildings, but after Benito Mussolini's rise to power in the 1920s, Naples became a center of urban renewal. The fascist leader's vision of a new Italian empire included plans to reimagine the country's cities as showplaces of imperial power. Naples became a centerpiece of Mussolini's attempts to renovate Italy's major cities with architecture that combined modernist and Roman-revival styles. Cook was seeing the fruits of the fascist leader's vision.

Cook also appreciated the natural beauty of Naples Bay and the rugged majesty of Mt. Vesuvius. He noted the smoke and fire emerging from the infamous volcano. Roughly five months after Cook described the mountain to Coach Rost, American forces found themselves dealing with another obstacle in addition to the Germans. For several days in March 1944, Mt. Vesuvius, just as it had in 79 AD when it buried Pompeii and Herculaneum, erupted, sending lava flows down the mountain and destroying several villages. Not surprisingly, it hit the nearby Pompeii Airfield, destroying dozens of B-25 Mitchell bombers of the 340th Bombardment Group.

Beyond the talk of Navy life and the scenery, Cook was not beyond his expressions of opinions on circumstances back home in the states. He vented to Rost on his annoyance with what he believed were the inexcusable labor grievances of American defense workers. In 1943 and 1944, labor unions representing several sectors of American manufacturing and services went on strike. Coal miners, steel workers, and railroad employees, among others, went on strikes that threatened war production. Sometimes the strikes ended at the urging of the War Department, but when the railroad union refused to resume operation of the routes in 1943, Secretary of War Stimson and the president ordered the Army to seize the railways and take over from the strikers. The strike ended, but tensions remained.

Locally, the employees of the Union Electric Plants in Venice and Cahokia, Illinois, went on strike in March 1944, which shut down the power plants and forced local defense manufacturing to halt production. The workers went back after the War Department resumed arbitration talks.

Cook, who sarcastically decries the striking defense workers, made it clear that he believed that men who remained back home should be grateful that they weren't fighting. Lumped with the "poor defense workers" were Cook's comments on the "zoot-suiters." The controversial flashy, baggy suits of the day were mostly associated with black and Latino men, and the fashion statement was generally sneered at by whites as being associated with hoodlums and criminals. In the summer of 1943, a group of 100 drunken sailors in Los Angeles started what became known as the Zoot Suit Riots. Upon seeing a group of 20 Mexican men attired in the suits, the sailors dragged them from cars and beat them. The violence was met with a counterattack over the next two days and spurred similar attacks in other American cities. St. Louis was spared the violence, but one angry St. Louis housewife wrote a letter to the *Globe-Democrat* proclaiming her outrage with the fashionable youths and questioning how they were exceeding fabric rationing. "Those zoot-suit kids! They have seen too many overdone gangster movies. Why is that? Why were the tailors of those suits allowed extra material?"

Cook's letter to Coach Rost allows us to see the complexity of the times and witness the destruction that war can inflict upon a city.

AT SEA

USS James O'Hara
c/o Fleet P.O.
New York, NY
Nov 10, 1943

Dear Coach: We are now running into a 40 knot Gale and a rough sea this ship is pitching and rolling something horrible. Thank God I'm not one of the many seasick on board. I don't know how long I'll hold out—forever if I feel as I do now, I guess.

I just returned from a trip to a forward hole—never saw such a funny sight before. We have a few soldiers on board and there sifting in their bunks holding a helmet between their knees. Occasionally they let fly into it, get up real into the head, clean their helmet, and then return to their bunks ready to begin a new heaving session. Really feel sorry for the boys.

I finally got to see Naples as I wanted to see it. About time after making so many trips there. It's the first city I've seen on this side of the pond that reminds me of an American city. They have many modernistic buildings, especially a postal office, train station, and auditorium. It's definitely a beautiful city, & I can readily see why so many tourists stop there. I really think there's isn't a more beautiful sight on water than the approach to Naples Harbor. The Isle of Capri to the left and Mt. Vesuvius with the volcano belching away smoke & fire to the right.

The Naples docks are a shamble. What our precision bombs didn't do the Nazis did. The harbor is filled with ships on their sides or those that just have their stacks and top decks showing.

The warehouses have been blown to bits. A lot of it we did, but what was left that night of any use to us was demolished before the Germans abandoned the city.

They even went so far as to blow up part of the water works & the rest they polluted. Most of the electric generators were damaged also. Once one gets away from the waterfront, however the damage isn't much at all.

It will soon be six months overseas for me. Time certainly has flown by. The only thing that makes me realize my length of stay is the amount of money I have saved and my occasional thoughts of home. I would like to see England before I return, spend a few months in the states and then head for the West Coast to see new lands.

I don't even know if I want to see the Invasion of France or the Netherlands. I swore I didn't care to take part in another invasion if I'd ever get out of the Salerno affair alive, but you know how the human mind is. Once you're away from the action a while it gets so that you don't want to miss any of the shows that have appearances of being top notch.

I have yet to run into any of my high school or college chums in this theater (Mediterranean). I guess most of them are on the West Coast.

My hat goes off to the army fighting north of Naples. If the civilian population of the US could only realize how rugged the terrain and how foul the weather (rain & snow constantly) I'm sure they'd understand why we've made such a slow progress.

How are the poor defense workers, strikers, and zoot suiters coming along? I do hope the government is treating the dear darlings nicely I'll guarantee you, Coach, that the government better not turn the disgruntled workers over to the servicemen overseas. I'm afraid there wouldn't be many of them left—Especially those on strike. If they and the zoot suitors are so bloody I wish they'd come over here and shed some of it

It's hard to visualize that another Xmas is almost here. If I'm not there to wish you and your family a "Merry Xmas & a Happy New Year" & personally, I do so now.

Regards to Mrs. Rost & the children.

As ever,

Joe

P.S. How did you make out this season?

Armored landing vehicles were produced at the St. Louis Car Company plant on North Broadway. *Collections of the Missouri Historical Society*

TANKS ROLL OFF THE LINES

There were four railroad car manufacturers in the St. Louis area in the early 20th century, and each of them played an important role in war production after Pearl Harbor. The largest of these was American Car and Foundry Company, a leading manufacturer of railroad cars of all kinds. The St. Louis region had three different divisions of ACF manufacturing equipment and armaments for the war. The Missouri Car and Foundry Company in St. Louis and the Madison Car Company in Madison, Illinois, switched from building railcars for American shipping companies to producing railcars for military transport of goods in Europe. Each division also produced sections of landing craft and dry docks for the US Navy.

A third division of the ACF was located in St. Charles, operating as the St. Charles Car Company. The downtown St. Charles foundry plant was a primary source of American light tanks and armored vehicles during the war. It received its first order from the military in 1941 to produce 329 light tanks. Production ramped up quickly as Roosevelt's quotas for defense production sought to catch up with the manufacturing capabilities of the Axis powers. By the end of the war, the US had built 102,000 tanks, of which over 17 percent were built by American Car and Foundry plants. The St. Charles factory held the distinction of producing 1,800 of those tanks.

In St. Louis, the St. Louis Car Company plant at 8000 North Broadway produced armored landing vehicles. It was a major production conversion for a company that made streetcars and passenger railcars, but it made the change and manufactured the landing vehicles used by American troops in both theaters of the war.

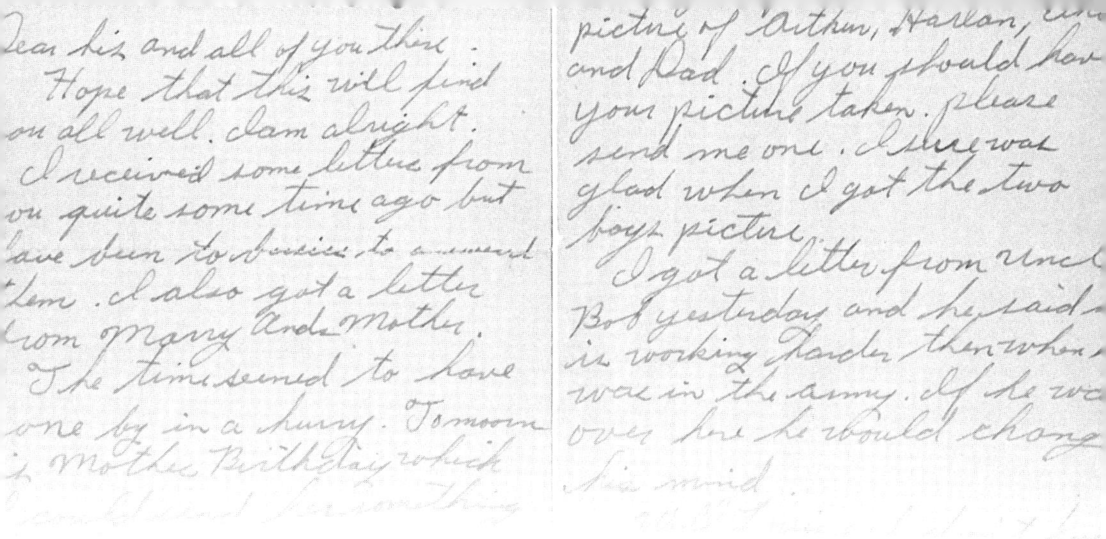

Dear Liz and all of you there.
Hope that this will find
you all well. I am alright.
I received some letters from
you quite some time ago but
have been too busy to answer
them. I also got a letter
from Mary And Mother.
The time seemed to have
gone by in a hurry. Tomorrow
is Mother Birthday which

picture of Arthur, Harlan, and
and Dad. If you should have
your picture taken. please
send me one. I sure was
glad when I got the two
boys picture.
I got a letter from Uncl
Bob yesterday and he said
is working harder then when
was in the army. If he was
over here he would chang
his mind.

Omar Kolkmeier letter, February 12, 1944. *St. Charles Historical Society*

"I AM STILL WORKING HARD LONG HOURS AND EVERY DAY CAN'T SAY WHAT I AM DOING THOUGH."

— SERGEANT OMAR KOLKMEIER, US ARMY

Harvester, Missouri, was a small farming community located in St. Charles County in the years before suburbanization transformed the landscape. It was a fitting name for a community surrounded by the wheat fields that once spread out across the county in all directions. By the 1880s, the majority of its residents, like a significant percentage of St. Charles County settlers at the time, were German immigrants. Some of these hardworking German families found abundance in farming, while others relied on their well-honed, old-world craftsmanship in skills such as cabinetmaking to make a living.

These newcomers laid down roots and created large families. While still retaining much of their German heritage (many families continued to speak more German than English in their homes), they embraced their new country and developed deep patriotism and a belief in the American dream.

The Kolkmeiers were one of these families. August and his wife lived in Harvester with their three sons and three daughters. One son, Omar, worked for his uncle's construction business at the time he was drafted in 1942. Upon entering the Army, Omar was sent to Fort Leonard Wood for basic training and then assigned to Company B of the 39th Combat Engineers.

Omar and the men of the 39th had their first taste of field experience in North Africa, where they were put through extensive combat training. But engineers would not experience real combat until they were loaded into the transport ship and prepared for Operation Husky, the invasion of Sicily in late July 1943. It was there that they would learn just how arduous their work would be.

The engineers set off from Tunisia for Sicily, making the relatively short crossing to the island, but the weather was not cooperating. As the landing craft were battered by rough seas and heavy winds, the men became seasick, not a condition to be in when preparing for battle. Many believed that the operation would be called off, but as they drew closer to their objective, the town of Gela, the weather calmed enough to proceed, and so the landing was on.

Under cover of darkness, the men lowered themselves into the waiting LCVPs (Landing Craft, Vehicles, Personnel) and waited for them to begin chugging toward the beaches. However, there was a delay, so the men stood waiting, jostled again by the waves, and once again seasickness began to overcome the troops. Finally, the boats began to move, but the LCVPs, scattered by the pounding

Sgt. Omar Kolkmeier. *St. Charles Historical Society*

waves, were now out of position. It was only through the guidance of their commander, Colonel William O. Darby of the Army Rangers, that they re-formed. This was performed by Darby's use of a megaphone to communicate with the LCVP pilots because radio communication was silenced. However, the approaching boats were detected when a searchlight caught sight of them.

The engineers were suddenly startled by the thunder of a tremendous explosion. The Germans had detonated explosives to blow up a large section of Gela's central pier, a pivotal landing point for the engineers. A group of Darby's men had previously landed with the objective of diffusing any such explosives, but they had failed to do so. Now a second light lit up the first wave of boats, and the Germans opened up on them with artillery.

In the next moments, the battle was fully engaged, with the Germans firing at the Americans and the US Navy shelling the battlements to knock out the searchlights. This was achieved, but the German artillery fire continued. One German shell scored a direct hit on one of the Company B LCVPs, causing it to capsize and throwing all into the churning seas. Miraculously, no one was killed as they all swam from the sinking boat. Then came another hang-up. One hundred yards from shore, another Company B craft hit a sandbar. There was no other recourse than to throw open the craft's landing deck, which immediately flooded the craft. The engineers spilled into the deep water and swam for shore. Once again, the entire group went unharmed, and they reached the beach.

Over the next few hours, there was a series of attacks and counterattacks that tested the engineers' resolve, but in the end, Gela was taken and the troops moved inland. Omar Kolkmeier endured it all. This, of course, was only the beginning of the engineer's trials in the Italian campaign.

From Gela, it was on to the Italian mainland, then toward Naples through the autumn of 1943. The next objective would be Anzio, code-named Operation Shingle.

The German command had thrown everything at the Anglo-American forces entering Italy. They were dug in and well equipped to stave off the Allied invaders. American and British troops had attempted to break through the German Gustav Line, but they faced some of Germany's best armored divisions and were hampered by torrential rains and flooded rivers blocking their way. So, the decision was made to launch an attack on the beaches of Anzio, 33 miles south of Rome.

A force of 36,000 Allied troops with 3,000 vehicles landed on the beaches. The attack on January 22, 1944, took the Germans by surprise as only two German battalions were present to counter the landing force, but a tactical error on the part of the Americans nearly caused the entire operation to fail. US Major John P. Lucas, the commander in charge, made the landing but chose not to proceed. He remained in place long enough for the Germans to take the high ground above Anzio. For weeks they shelled the beaches and the town.

Allied troops were caught under the German shelling, and a long stalemate began. Throughout March, new Allied troops continued to land, as the fighting diminished into skirmishes. It was during this action that Omar Kolkmeier, who had survived the perilous landing at Gela, was killed on March 26, 1944. His last letter home had been sent on March 18. It mentioned his landing on Anzio Beach. It was there that he is presumed to have fallen, likely killed by the German shelling in the days after his arrival.

Back in Harvester, the Kolkmeiers learned of their son's death on May 20. Eventually, Omar's remains arrived home. His family were congregants of Freidens Church near Harvester, and he was laid to rest in the church's graveyard now located within St. Charles.

In one of Omar's last letters home, he wrote the following.

> Somewhere in Italy
>
> Feb. 12, 1944
>
> Dear Sis and all of you there:
>
> Hope that this will find you all well. I am alright.
>
> I received some letters from you quite some time ago but have been too busy to answer them. I also got a letter from Marry and Mother.
>
> The time seemed to have gone by in a hurry. Tomorrow is Mothers Birthday which I could send her something but that is impossible.
>
> I am still working hard long hours and every day can't say what I am doing though. Which I could. Ethel sended me her picture some time ago. Bo it really was a good picture. I have a picture of Arthur, Harlan, Ethel, and Dad. If you should have your picture taken, please send me one. I sure was glad when I got the tow boys picture.
>
> I got a letter from Uncle Bob yesterday and he said he is working harder then when he was in the army. If he was over here he would change his mind.
>
> Well Louise I don't what else to write so tell every body Hello.
>
> Always more than glad to get your letter.
>
> Your brother,
>
> Omar

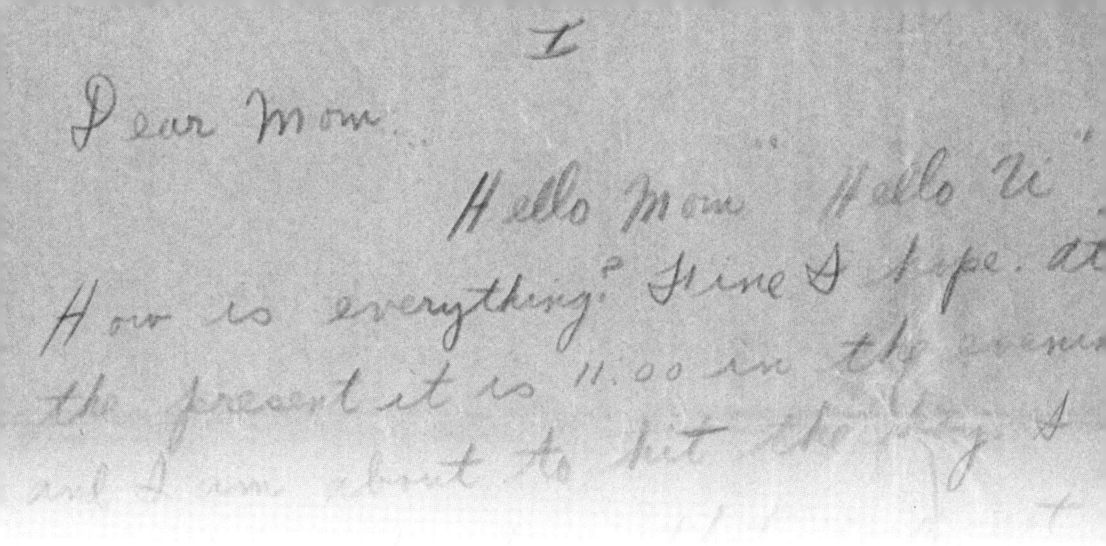
Dear Mom:
Hello Mom
How is everything? Fine I hope.
the present it is 11:00 in the
and I am about to hit the

Kenneth Risch letter, May 23, 1943. *Judy Kaufman*

"JOHN HAS BEEN THROUGH HELL." — THE SAGA OF THE RISCH BROTHERS

John Kenneth Risch and Kenneth John Risch were twins. Johnny and Kenny grew up with their younger brother, Tommy, and sisters, Marie and Elvira, on Dalton Street near Reber Park in St. Louis's South City neighborhoods.

Kenneth was the first of the Risch sons to marry. He married Mary shortly before the war. Later, in a letter to his mother while he was away at basic training, he would say that Mary was "such a good wife and mother" and implored his mom that if "you hear anyone talk about her, you tell them off."

John was the first son to join the Army. He enlisted in 1942 and was sent to Camp Gruber. Thereafter, he was assigned to the artillery. His duty would take him to some of the fiercest fighting of the war, the invasion of Italy and later the Battle of the Bulge. He would do his time as a "cannoneer on the long tom," a 155-millimeter caliber field gun capable of firing 100-pound shells 14 miles. It was a monster of a gun, and it did its job against the Germans like no other.

At Anzio, the Allies and Germans rained shells on each other for weeks in the first months of 1944. The Associated Press reported on February 22, 1944, that "allied and German heavy guns pounded each other's line and heavy artillery dueling on the Anzio beachhead today as both sides recuperated from unbroken days of bitter fighting and prepared for further battle." The fighting was hard and the advance slow. AP reporter Edward Kennedy, who was embedded with the Army at Anzio, wrote that the action he witnessed was "no brilliant victory, no triumphal entry into Rome, but a hard, grueling struggle against the odds."

As a private in the artillery, John was in the thick of it. The deafening roar of the Allied heavy artillery and the constant shelling in return from the Germans left both sides weary, and the death tolls rose. Needless to say, it would have been unnerving for anyone.

The Battle of Anzio, launched on January 22, 1944, was one

Pvt. John Risch. *Judy Kaufman*

of the most daring and controversial operations of the Italian Campaign during World War II. This amphibious assault aimed to bypass the heavily fortified German Gustav Line and pave the way for an Allied advance toward Rome. Though ultimately successful, the battle was marked by a prolonged stalemate, fierce resistance, and significant loss of life.

By late 1943, the Allied advance in Italy had slowed. The Gustav Line, anchored by the stronghold at Monte Cassino, presented an almost impenetrable barrier. In an effort to outflank German defenses and hasten the capture of Rome, the Allies devised Operation Shingle. The plan involved landing a substantial force at Anzio, a coastal town south of Rome, to threaten the German rear and draw their forces away from the Gustav Line.

The amphibious landings at Anzio began under the cover of darkness. Supported by naval bombardments and air cover, Allied forces encountered minimal initial resistance. The German defenders, under Field Marshal Albert Kesselring, were caught off guard. By the end of the first day, the Allies had secured a beachhead with minimal casualties.

However, General Lucas's decision to consolidate and fortify the beachhead rather than push inland immediately allowed the Germans to regroup. This cautious approach drew criticism from Allied commanders, including General Mark W. Clark and British Prime Minister Winston Churchill, who famously remarked, "I had hoped we were hurling a wildcat onto the shore, but all we got was a stranded whale."

As German reinforcements poured into the area, the beachhead became a cauldron of intense fighting. The Allies faced fierce artillery barrages, tank assaults, and counterattacks. The harsh winter weather added to the soldiers' misery, turning the battlefield into a muddy quagmire.

The broader context of the Italian Campaign further complicated the situation. While the Allies struggled at Anzio, the Fifth Army was engaged in a grueling battle at Monte Cassino.

Monte Cassino, however, remained a significant obstacle. The ancient Benedictine monastery atop Monte Cassino became a focal point of fierce fighting, as German forces used its strategic position to hold off the Allies. Between January and May 1944, the battle for Monte Cassino raged with multiple assaults and heavy bombardments, culminating in the destruction of the abbey and the surrounding village of Cassino. The ruins bore witness to the devastating cost of war and the determination of Allied forces.

After months of stalemate, the Allies launched a coordinated offensive in May 1944. Combining pressure on the Gustav Line with a renewed push from Anzio, they succeeded in breaking through German defenses. On June 4, 1944, Allied forces entered Rome, marking a significant milestone in the Italian Campaign.

Despite its ultimate success, the Battle of Anzio remains controversial. Critics argue that delays and missteps prolonged the conflict, while others highlight the bravery and resilience of the soldiers who endured tremendous hardships. The destruction of Monte Cassino and the village of Cassino further underscore the heavy toll of the campaign on soldiers and civilians alike.

After the battle, John returned to the ruins of Monte Cassino, where he picked up a green stone from the abbey's remains and sent it to his grandmother with the note:

> Mom, This cut stone is from the Monte Cassino. I went through Cassino before I left Italy. Most of the boys that fought there had to go back to look at it. There is nothing left of the town. You can see by this gold that it must have been old and beautiful. It sure was a shame.

John was still "Somewhere in Italy" in May 1944, but that would soon change with the landing of the Allied invasion of Normandy. He would be transferred to the French front.

Meanwhile, John's brothers had also entered the military. Kenneth and Tommy both enlisted in the Army Air Corps. Together, they were sent to train at Sheppard Airfield in Wichita Falls, Texas. When their training was finished, they joined the thousands of American airmen stationed in Great Britain. Although scattered far and wide, all the brothers tried their best to keep in contact with each other. Ken was aware of John's battle experiences and expressed concern in a letter to his mother in October 1944.

> "Somewhere in England"
>
> Thursday, October 26, 1944
>
> Dear Mom,
>
> "Hello Mom" How is everything with you? Fine I hope. I hope you're feeling a lot better. I got a letter from Johnny the other day. I think it's about time for him to go back. He sure has been through hell. I'd give anything to see him. And who knows, I might yet. If there's any way that I can, I will . . . Well, Mom, I'm in England 13 months now and I'm ready to go back. It takes a thing like a war to make a person appreciate the old USA.
>
> Well, Mom, I'll say goodnight. Take good care of yourself. I'll send my picture to you the same time I send Mary's. Tell Vi to write.
>
> As always, your son, Ken

For his part, John also wrote to his mother in October. His account to her was more subdued than what Ken had alluded to in his letter, but John did mention that he was tired and still in the thick of the fighting.

> "Somewhere in France"
>
> Sunday October 8th 1944
>
> Dear Mom,
>
> Well here it is Sunday morning but just another day in the army. I pulled guard duty last night so I'm a little tired. We are really kept busy over here now and the Kraut is

> catching hell as usual. I hope the big day isn't too far away. I would not like to be on the receiving end. I had a surprise this morning. My old outfit is right here with me. I haven't seen them yet. But we'll look them up. Tom Hughes won't be here. If you remember he was discharged with a bad stomach. But I'll see the rest of the boys. It will surprise them to find me back in a service battery. I've LED quite an exciting life when for four months I was a cannoneer on the Long Tom. That sure was rough and I would say that the job called for a little . . . credit. Well enough of that stuff. I hope you are feeling fine.
>
> Well, I'll close for now and write again in a day or so. Write soon. Send me shave lotion and either you or the girls make some cookies and send me some.

John would write again a few weeks later to offer his mother advice on the upcoming 1944 presidential election. He implored her not to vote for the Republican nominee Thomas Dewey over President Roosevelt. "Before I forget," he wrote her, "I would not vote for Dewey. I know how he is with people that are not of his class and he is a Slug Head."

In the same letter, John also spoke of another topic that was all the buzz in St. Louis that year, the 1944 St. Louis Browns versus Cardinals World Series. The 41st World Series was the first-ever championship matchup between the two St. Louis teams. "Mom, I heard all of the World Series. I believe I told you in my last letter. It was a swell series. It's too bad the Brownies could not have won." John was obviously a Browns fan and disappointed by their loss, but listening to the game must have felt a bit like being at home. Broadcasting from Sportsman's Park, it beamed across Armed Forces Radio to soldiers and sailors across the world and all the ships at sea. It would have been a perfect respite from the tiresome fighting.

As 1944 came to a close, things would go from bad to worse for those fighting in France and Belgium. The Germans were suffering heavy losses as the Americans fought village to village. John wrote in early December that "I'm feeling fine and getting close to Heine Land. I can smell the kraut." Making light of it was probably the best way to handle the stressful conditions that the Allied troops were enduring. "Believe me," he continued, "Germany isn't standing still. They are putting up some good resistance."

As the Germans were pushed closer and closer to their own borders, Hitler decided to make one last drive to push the Allies back from the Fatherland. He waited for the weather to turn cold and overcast, knowing that the Allies would have a difficult time running bombing sorties in such difficult conditions. Then, just before Christmas, he ordered SS Panzer divisions to make a race for the Ardennes forests of Belgium in an attempt to draw off American forces from their advance toward Germany. His strategy worked, as the Allies were completely caught off guard by the move. Thus began the Battle of the Bulge.

On December 19, Ken wrote to his mother, "Mom, have you heard from Johnny lately? I haven't. I hope I do soon. Things look pretty rough in his territory." Things in Belgium were rough indeed. Units such as the 933rd Field Artillery Battalion were rushed from France to engage the Germans in the frigid Belgian and Alsatian countryside. Many of the units were not prepared for the cold and were fighting in regular uniforms rather than with protective winter coats. Temperatures dropped into the single digits, and men were freezing to death.

The Air Force was grounded by the bad weather, and the Germans took full advantage of the situation. They also employed tactics such as seizing American equipment and uniforms and using them to penetrate even further under disguise. One of the most outrageous war crimes committed by the German SS troops against the Americans took place during the Bulge. It involved the taking of a field artillery unit much like John's.

On the first day of the German offensive, a field artillery observation battalion was cut off by advancing German troops and unable to get back behind the Allied lines. When they became pinned down, they had no other option but to surrender. The Nazi Waffen SS unit took them prisoner and brought them to a field to join other American prisoners. There were 113 American prisoners assembled. An SS officer arrived, pointed a gun at one of the American soldiers, and immediately the Waffen SS guards machine-gunned the American prisoners. They also killed several civilians who had witnessed the attack. Of the 113, 84 were killed. Those who survived had played dead or hidden under the bodies of their comrades. Among the victims of the Malmedy Massacre was a citizen of Franklin County, Missouri, T/5 Raymond Heitman, 197th Anti-Aircraft Battalion of Union, Missouri.

It wasn't until the weather broke that the Americans would effectively counter the German operation. In the end, it was a worthless gamble for the Nazi leadership; they could not have sustained the attack even if they had been successful because their fuel supplies were exhausted. Many of the advancing Panzer divisions simply had to stop because they had run out of gas. Hitler's last attempt at revenge had cost the lives of thousands, including 11,609 members of the American Seventh Army.

In January 1945, John had made it through the Bulge. The family was relieved to hear from him. He wrote his mother on January 20 to tell her about his situation. A friend of his was trying to get back to the United States, and he had apparently promised John to let Louise know how John was doing. "I hope by now you know my situation. I'll tell you at present it's rough. If my buddy made it back to the states, then you should have an idea of what I'm doing. I hope this damn thing ends soon."

In the end, all three of the Risch boys made it home alive, but the cost of war is sometimes not entirely apparent. The soldiers who returned home in one piece considered themselves lucky. They had survived to tell the stories, but though they may not have been injured physically, the toll of what they had lived through was often more mental than physical. Combat changes people. No one can be the same person after watching humans actively working to kill each other, be they friend or foe. The soldiers of World War II were just as human as the soldiers of any other conflict, and they too would suffer what was known then as battle fatigue but is now recognized as Post-Traumatic Stress Disorder (PTSD).

Contemporary studies have shown that the mental effects of combat sometimes don't appear for years or even decades. Studies of elderly World War II veterans found that later life events such as losing a spouse or experiencing a serious illness can trigger trauma-induced memories and behaviors. Years may pass, but sadly the memories remain.

Modern health professionals no longer question the existence of PTSD, but it was largely dismissed by many physicians and the larger public prior to the 1980s. Work with Vietnam, Gulf War, and Iraq War veterans resulted in a much better understanding of the psychological effects of combat. Today, much of the remaining controversy revolves around whether PTSD is diagnosed enough among veterans, given the troubling number of suicides within the veteran community.

The final piece of the Johnny and Kenny war story came years later. Both returned home to St. Louis, but neither, especially Johnny, was ever the same. Their niece, Judy Kaufman, remembers the good times the family had when she was a child growing up in the 1950s. The two men would often entertain the family during events like family picnics. They had beautiful singing voices and harmonized perfectly, recalled Judy.

Both men were married and had families. They were working, though having trouble maintaining jobs. Then one day, to everyone's amazement, the two brothers, Johnny and Kenny, left their families, took to the road, and never returned. Judy believes both men suffered war trauma, PTSD, but it was simply not understood then. A brother-in-law, a fellow World War II veteran and former Marine, Bud Moore, could never understand or forgive them for abandoning their families.

Only those soldiers who had experienced the violence and horrors of Anzio, D-Day, the Bulge, Iwo Jima, Okinawa, and countless other engagements could truly understand what the soldiers of World War II survived. They had to live the rest of their lives remembering what they could not unsee and dealing with the pain of loss. Time sometimes cannot erase such tragedy nor lessen the trauma.

John Kenneth Risch is buried far from home in Greenwood Cemetery in Superior, Wisconsin. Kenneth John Risch is buried in Fort Snelling National Cemetery in Minnesota.

Tommy Risch remained in St. Louis. He is buried in Jefferson Barracks National Cemetery.

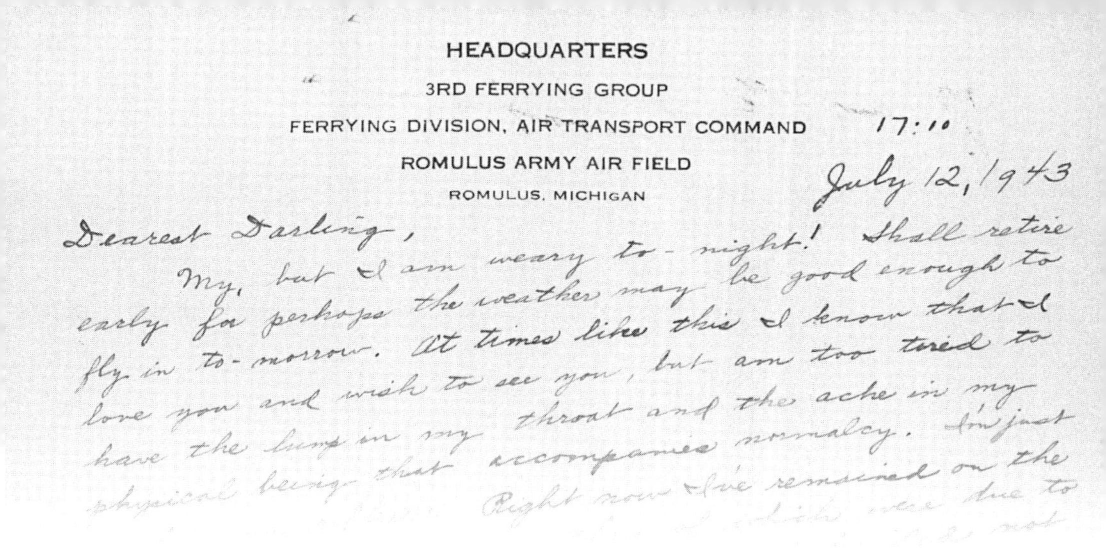

HEADQUARTERS
3RD FERRYING GROUP
FERRYING DIVISION, AIR TRANSPORT COMMAND
ROMULUS ARMY AIR FIELD
ROMULUS, MICHIGAN

17:10
July 12, 1943

Dearest Darling,

My, but I am weary to-night! Shall retire early for perhaps the weather may be good enough to fly in to-morrow. At times like this I know that I love you and wish to see you, but am too tired to have the lump in my throat and the ache in my physical being that accompanies normalcy. I'm just [illegible] Right now I've remained on the [illegible] due to [illegible]

Adela Riek Scharr letter, July 12, 1943. *St. Louis Public Library Manuscript Division*

"WE ARE GETTING A GOOD PICTURE OF THE WAR AND OUR SMALL PART IN IT."
— ADELA RIEK SCHARR, WOMEN AIRFORCE SERVICE PILOT

During World War II, the United States faced a shortage of pilots to ferry aircraft from factories to military bases. To address this, the Army Air Forces (AAF) established the Women's Auxiliary Ferrying Squadron (WAFS) in September 1942, appointing Nancy Harkness Love as its commander. This program enlisted experienced female pilots to transport aircraft within the United States, freeing male pilots for combat roles.

Simultaneously, the Women's Flying Training Detachment (WFTD), led by Jacqueline Cochran, was formed to train women pilots for various noncombat duties. In August 1943, these two organizations merged to create the Women Airforce Service Pilots (WASP), with Cochran as the director and Love overseeing ferrying operations. The WASP program expanded women's roles in aviation, allowing them to serve as flight instructors, tow targets for live anti-aircraft practice, transport cargo, and test experimental aircraft.

The WASP program's ferrying and transportation services played a key role in the war effort, ensuring that aircraft reached their destinations efficiently. Despite their contributions, the WASPs were considered civilians and did not receive military benefits during the war. It wasn't until 1977 that they were granted veteran status, recognizing their invaluable service to the nation.

One of the WASPs who achieved an almost celebrity status was Adela Riek Scharr of St. Louis. She was an accomplished pilot who took up flying in the 1930s when she was working as a teacher in the St. Louis Public Schools. It began in 1935 when she took her first lessons at Lambert Field by flying a Wright J5 Travel-Air, then Adela took a vacation to San Diego and received lessons from the seasoned fliers at Ryan Air, the company that built aviator Charles Lindbergh's *Spirit of St. Louis*. By 1937, she had her pilot's license. Soon she was giving lessons at Lambert. It was while working as an instructor that she met Harold Scharr, who signed up as a student pilot. The couple married, and Adela continued her work as an instructor, but ironically, while changing gender norms allowed women to be pilots in the 1930s, very old standards for women teaching in the school systems prohibited married women from teaching. Adela was forced to resign her teaching job, and flying became her full-time job.

In 1940, Adela made the news as the first female commercial pilot in St. Louis. She told the *Globe-Democrat* that her next goal was to start a women's flying club, which she did soon after. When the war broke out, her skills as a pilot were immediately recognized by the military as a possible asset to the war effort. Adela's first service with the Army came from the perceived need to create local air squadrons that would serve to defend against any enemy aircraft that might make it as far as America's heartland. Provided with the less-than-flattering name Powder Puff Squadrons, Adela was made the squadron commander for the St. Louis region. Soon after, she was recruited to join the Women's Aircraft Ferry Service (WAFS) and would start shuttling fighter aircraft from factories and bases across the country in 1942.

Adela's letters tell of her flights and the experiences of other WASPs. She was flying some of the most sophisticated aircraft of the day: P-39s, P-40s, P-1s, and P-47s. In *Sisters in the Sky*, Adela's memoir of her time as a WASP, she tells of her experience flying these various pursuit planes. One of the more amusing stories occurred one day while flying a P-51 from Scott Field to Pittsburgh. WASPs had a strict dress code and had to keep their shirts clean and wrinkle-free. The cockpits of the aircraft were cramped and hot, so it wasn't unusual for the women to remove their shirts while flying. After landing in Pittsburgh and picking up a new plane to ferry, she once again removed her shirt and began taxiing toward the runway. As she passed another plane, she heard the pilot exclaim into the open mic, "My God! She hasn't any clothes on!" Adela hit the throttle and got out of there as fast as she could, not because of the exposure but because she feared being reprimanded for not being in uniform. When she landed again, she parked her plane at the farthest end of the row of Mustangs sitting on the tarmac. As the lineman who helped guide the plane on the ground walked up, "I held up my shirt for the lineboy to see, put my right finger to my lips and winked. The fellow laughed with me and moved from sight. A lady needs some privacy while dressing."

The WASPs faced challenges every day in the air, but they also had to overcome the prejudice of those who did not believe that women belonged in the cockpit. The women were subjected to greater scrutiny than men. Adela held her own, and her accounts reflect largely positive experiences in the service, but Adela's letters hint that some women, whether due to skill or temperament, did not always have the same rapport with those in command over flying privileges, as pointed out in this letter to Harold.

17: 00

July 12, 1943

Darling,

My, but I am weary tonight! Shall retire early for perhaps the weather may be good enough to fly in tomorrow. At times like this I know that I love you and wish to see you, but I am too tired to have the lump in my throat and the ache in my physical being that encompasses normalcy. I'm just dead in my reflexes. Right now I've remained on the ground about four days—three of which were due to that normal physical disturbance. I decided not to fly the P-39 at a time like that. Okay?

10 new burdens will be added tomorrow. I'm delighted in the attitude of those I got last as they are willing to work to help me carry on. When I get to deliver those P-39 (thru home, I hope) there'll be some lil gals to carry the job while I'm away.

Well, well it looks like I'll be the only woman flying pea-shooter for a while. Donnie made such a bad exhibition a la Helen Hastman style at the eighth hour or so that she had to be jerked off. She pleaded for several hours, but the men's minds were made-up. They feared she'd break a plane, her neck, or both, I promise you that I'll be so careful that chances will not be too great that I get hurt.

I'll be seeing you as soon as I can, dear. And remember I love you forever.

Your loving wife,

Del

WASPs were allowed to fly only stateside, but this did not mean that their experiences could be any less harrowing than their male combat fighter compatriots. Besides ferrying aircraft, some of the women participated in training exercises for antiaircraft gunnery units. They would tow drones behind lumbering B-25 bombers for the men on the ground to aim at for target practice. On several occasions, the men mistakenly thought they were supposed to shoot the planes, not the drones, thereby injuring the women pilots.

Crashes also took the lives of some of the women, including Hazel Ying Lee, one of only two Chinese American pilots to serve during World War II. Hazel, 32, was killed while attempting to land a P-63 Kingcobra in Great Falls, Montana. A miscommunication between air traffic controllers caused her to collide with another plane.

Air traffic control was still in its infancy during World War II. The operation depended largely on visual sighting and radio communications between the control tower and the pilots. Adela had her own close call one day while attempting to land a P-51C Mustang at the airfield in Long Beach, California. Her experience demonstrated that air traffic controllers' communications were important both in the air and on the ground.

Adela recounted in *Sisters in the Sky* that she arrived in the airspace over Long Beach only to discover that there was heavy air traffic all around her. The control tower was busy juggling all the planes circling within the airspace. "I went around and around, making a smaller pattern than the others," she recalled. "There were a few near collisions that I could see." Finally, she was given permission to land. The P-51 touched down on the runway, but the Mustang's cockpit sits high, and as she was making the landing roll, she was blind to the fact that repairs were being made to the runway. The air traffic controllers had not warned her about the construction that had shortened the runway by several feet. Luckily, she saw it and hit the brakes, but not before running her wheels into the gravel. Adela and the plane came out fine, but it showed how easily human error can result in disaster.

Adela had a unique job, and she loved what she did, but it came at a cost; she was separated from her husband. Each letter to Harold, who had enlisted in the Navy and served as an officer in the Pacific, expressed her desire to see and be with him.

V-Mail

A.R. Scharr, WASP
6th Ferrying Group
Long Beach, California

Dear Darling Harold,

Out at Radar trying to write on a step cause if I don't soon, I may neglect you again today. Hope you're not worrying. I love you just as always and really miss you, especially when a lot of nice things happen to me. Yesterday a group of us went to Silver Springs where the Tarzan pictures were taken, where Ross Allen has a snake farm and milks venom from snakes, and where a lot of under water pictures are taken.

We are getting a good picture of the war and our small part in it. Makes us understand also how we have a chance of winning, which is hard to figure unless you know how a war is run.

Wish you were here to hold my hand at the cinemas.

Your ever loving,

Del

Adela's service did not end with the war. She was commissioned as a major in the Air Force Reserves in the 1950s. Today, women fly jets large and small in the military and for airlines, but this wasn't always the case. In part, they have Adela to thank for breaking the barrier because in 1961, she was the first woman to fly a C-135 Stratolifter, the four-engine transport plane based off the civilian Boeing 707 airliner. No woman had flown a jet of this size and power before her. It was a test, approved by Cold War generals, to see if women could handle the heavy aircraft in case a third world war demanded a unit like the WASPs to be reinstated. Adela passed the test and helped open the skies to a new generation of women pilots.

Besides changes to the friendly skies, the education system was also coming into the 20th century. In the 1950s, St. Louis Public Schools changed its policies concerning married teachers, and

Adela went back to the classroom. She taught until her retirement in 1972. Adela Riek Scharr lived to be 90 years old. She passed away in St. Louis in 1998.

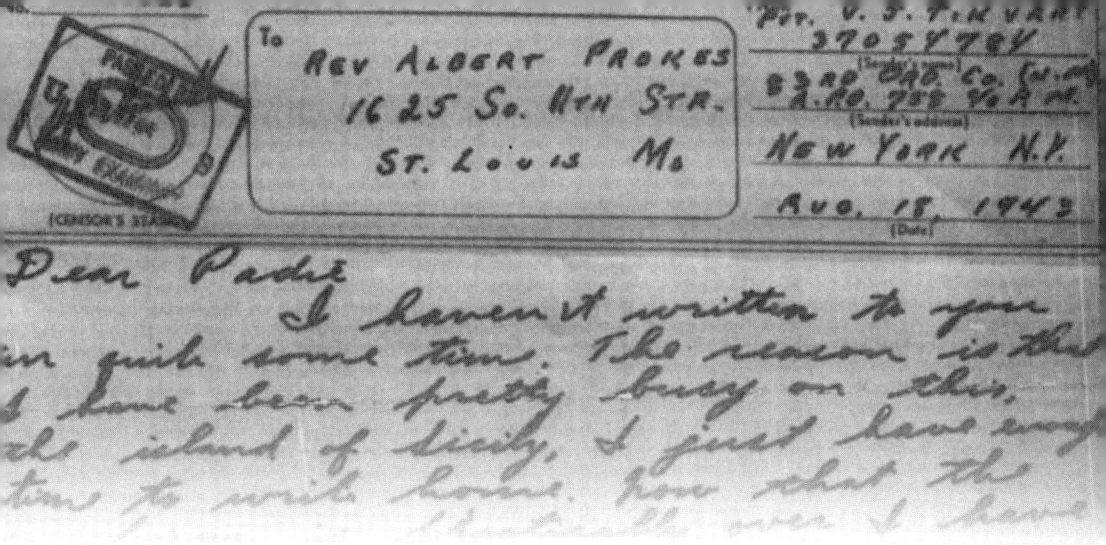

To
Rev Albert Prokes
1625 So. 11th Str.
St. Louis Mo

New York N.Y.
Aug. 18, 1943

Dear Padre
I haven't written to you in quite some time. The reason is that I have been pretty busy on this, the island of Sicily, I just have enough time to write home. Now that the

T/5 Vincent J. Tikvart V-mail, August 18, 1943. *The State Historical Society of Missouri*

"THERE ARE A LOT OF EMOTIONS THAT TAKE COMMAND OF A SOLDIER."
— TEC 5 VINCENT J. TIKVART, US ARMY

Vincent Tikvart was a kid from South St. Louis. His life and upbringing were very much like many of his South City neighbors. Vincent was the son of immigrants and grew up in the family home at 1511 Picker Street. His mother, Antoinette, was born in Bohemia and his father, Joseph, in Plzen, now in the Czech Republic, then still part of the Austro-Hungarian Empire. The couple had three sons: Joseph, Anthony, and Vincent.

The Tikvarts were members of the Parish of St. John Nepomuk Catholic Church in the city's Soulard neighborhood. This parish was the heart of St. Louis's Czech and Slovak communities. Foremost among the priests of St. John Nepomuk was Reverend Albert Prokes, the son of a St. Louis blacksmith and also a member of a family of Czech descent. Father Prokes was ordained in 1926 by Cardinal John J. Glennon, and by 1942, he was named administrator of the St. John Nepomuk parish.

The lives of the Tikvart boys would be entwined with the parish and consequently with Father Prokes, who might also have served as a surrogate father for the young men whose father had died in 1933. St. John Nepomuk was part of the fabric of the community, and its very presence loomed large. It bridged the New World and the Old and kept traditions alive. In a time when the world seemed to be changing, and growing more threatening, the church was a firm symbol of community and faith.

The times were changing, sometimes for the better, but increasingly it appeared that the world was becoming a scarier place. Sabers were rattling in Europe. The Tikvarts were fully American, but the old country still held a large place in their hearts. Given the family's ties to Czechoslovakia, they were naturally disturbed by Hitler's talk of taking the Sudetenland in 1938. Hitler had declared that he wanted to free the region's minority German population from the persecution and oppression that they suffered under Czech control. He sought to annex the territory to Germany. After taking Austria, occupying the Sudetenland was the next step in the German dictator's plan to begin conquering land to build the Third Reich.

Anthony took it upon himself to write a letter to the opinion page of the *St. Louis Post-Dispatch* condemning Hitler's supporters, who repeated the dictator's claims of supposed oppression of those minority Germans living in the Czech region. "The Sedetens enjoy numerous privileges in the democratic form of the Czechoslovakian Government, which they would not get in the fanatic Hilterdom," Anthony decried. "When a slight difference arises in the Sedeten territory, such as a minor drunken saloon brawl—which happens every day even in this country—they immediately cry they are persecuted. It is true that Hitler does not want the Czechs. He wants the rich agricultural and iron lands."

Three weeks after Anthony's letter was printed, German troops entered the Czech territory and took the Sudetenland. It was only fitting then that Anthony and Vincent would join the Army when Germany declared war on the US four years later. The Tikvart boys would fight not only for their country but also to destroy the fascist authoritarians holding the land of their forefathers. Vincent would find himself assigned to a tank unit, while Anthony became a member of the airborne engineers.

When the war broke out, Prokes became very active in leading community activities to support the war effort, especially in support of the young men of the parish who had enlisted or been drafted.

During the same summer as Prokes's elevation to administrator of the parish, members of a group of parents whose sons were serving in the war established a committee called "The Home Front" whose purpose was to collect the addresses of the more than 80 young men who were in the service from the parish so they could continue to correspond with home. The committee, which grew to almost 200 parishioners, also provided care packages to the men such as Christmas presents, boxes of candies and toiletries, and, of course, the ever-sought-after cigarettes. Included in each package or mailed to each serviceman was a copy of the *Messenger*, a publication containing church news, community news, and letters received from the servicemen printed by the Home Front Committee.

In addition to the *Messenger*, Reverend Prokes also kept up correspondence with many of the servicemen, who wrote to thank him for the church bulletins and the gifts, but also to thank him for the guidance and support he had provided to them during their years with the parish. Prokes kept the letters, and they are now in the collections of The State Historical Society of Missouri.

There is a common theme to many of the letters: first, expressions of thanks for all the support, followed by descriptions of their life in the military. Yet standing out among the letters is the one written by Vincent Tikvart in 1943. Tick, as he refers to himself, had endured the bitter fighting of the Invasion of Sicily. Code-named Operation Husky, the invasion of the Italian island of Sicily began on July 10, 1943. Vincent's tank unit served as part of the Seventh Army led by General George S. Patton.

The Germans initially provided little resistance when the main forces hit the beaches, but after several days, the Germans rallied as they attempted to hold off the Allies long enough to evacuate the island.

The invasion was over in 39 days, but with a toll of 9,700 American lives taken in the fighting. It was the first taste of real combat for many of the soldiers. Many of the soldiers in Operation Husky had been on duty in North Africa and had seen combat, but not on the scale of the Sicilian actions. Tikvart's letter to Father Prokes is dated one day after the Sicilian invasion was declared over and secured. The Germans had fled to the mainland, and now the Allied troops could take a breather.

Vincent's letter is emblematic of one that a soldier might be willing to write only to his priest. You get a sense that he was struggling a bit to deal with the violence and hardships he had witnessed. During the thick of the fighting, Vincent likely experienced a level of fear and emotion unlike any time before. Now he was seeking consolation and reassurance from a clergyman he knew and trusted.

V-Mail

August 18, 1943

Dear Padre

I haven't written to you in quite some time. The reason is that I have been pretty busy on this, the island of Sicily, I just have enough time to write home. Now that the campaign is practically over I have more time.

I have seen many of the horrors of war, I won't go in to detail about it though. It makes a man think of God and his many blessings, also makes him want to continue living more than ever. There are a lot of emotions that take command of a soldier, hate and fear being two of the most common of them.

I have received the latest Messengers and enjoyed reading them more than I did at any other time. They made me feel a lot better to know that we over here are protecting that kind of life.

Yours sincerely,

"Tick"

We don't have Father Prokes's reply to Vincent, but it seems likely he answered Vincent's letter with words of solace.

The fight to oust the Germans from Italy became a bitter struggle once the Allies landed on the mainland. Vincent fought on, and somewhere in the mass of soldiers in the Italian campaigns, so did Anthony. They were both stationed in the same country but not able to see each other. Finally, during the final weeks of the war in March 1945, Vincent and Anthony had a reunion in Naples. The story made the *Post-Dispatch*. It was a happy ending that everyone could appreciate.

Tec 5 Vincent Tikvart passed away in 1984. He was a retired postal worker. Sergeant Anthony F. Tikvart, a lifelong member of VFW Post #1102, passed away in 2003. The brothers are buried in Jefferson Barracks National Cemetery.

Members of the St. John Nepomuk Parish established the Home Front Committee in 1942. The committee formed to facilitate correspondence with servicemen from the parish and provide them with care packages from home. *Collections of the Missouri Historical Society*

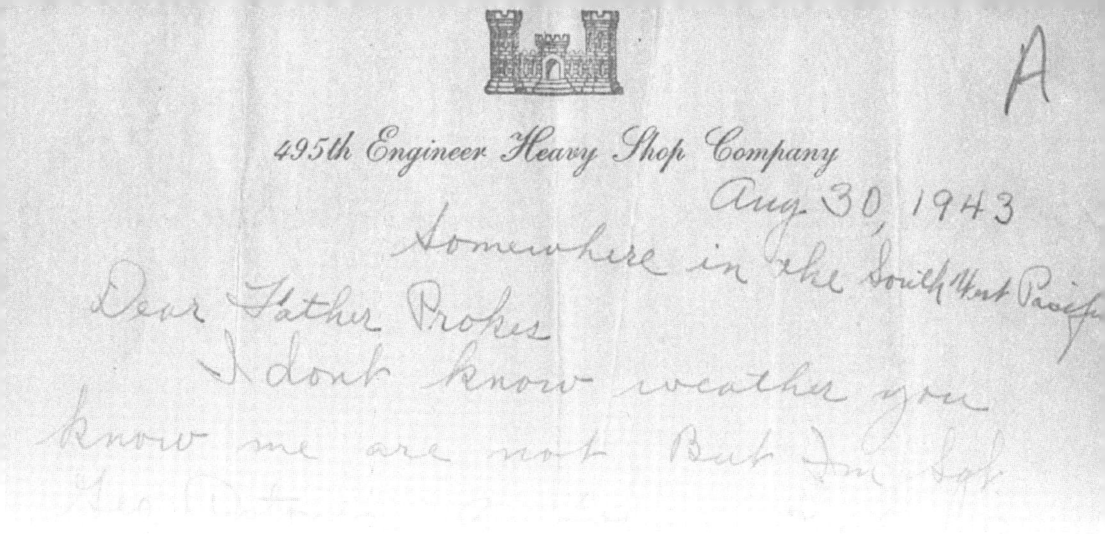
495th Engineer Heavy Shop Company

Aug. 30, 1943

Somewhere in the South West Pacific

Dear Father Prokes

I dont know weather you know me are not But Im Sgt

Tech Sergeant George Antonic letter, August 30, 1943. *The State Historical Society of Missouri*

"THANK YOU ALL FOR REMEMBERING US ORPHANS."

— TECH SERGEANT GEORGE ANTONIC, US ARMY

Father Albert Prokes of St. John Nepomuk served the church in more than one capacity. Besides his duties to the St. John Nepomuk parish, he was the guardian of the Hessoun Orphanage in Fenton, Missouri. In this capacity, Father Prokes was the orphan's advocate and legal representative but also the closest thing that many children had to a parent. The responsibility of caring for orphans is a difficult task at any time, but Father Prokes was in charge during the years of the Great Depression when the orphanages often became caretakers for the children of families struggling to care for their own children. It was not uncommon for parents, especially single mothers or parents of large families, to send their children to orphanages temporarily because of financial strain. Children were sometimes abandoned as well by parents who no longer wanted or believed that they could support their children. At the height of the Depression, a US government report noted that 144,000 children were living in orphanages. This was the highest number ever recorded.

The Hessoun Bohemian Catholic Orphanage was founded in years just before the outbreak of World War I. A committee of Bohemian immigrants under the direction of the Catholic Church purchased a 100-acre farm along Smizer Mill Road near Fenton, Missouri. The institution operated for just over four decades and was home to hundreds of children.

Among the many orphans taking refuge at Hessoun in the early 1930s was George Albert Antonic and his brother, Stephan. Under the care of Father Prokes and the sisters, George received an elementary education. He attended one year of high school, but Antonic had the good fortune to find employment, guidance, and training with the help of John Fabick Sr. of John Fabick Truck Company of Fenton. In his letter to Prokes, Antonic credits Fabick for sending him to diesel mechanics school and teaching him the trade. It was a skill that he carried forward when he entered the US Army in 1943.

The Army utilized Antonic's skills and knowledge and assigned him to an engineer's unit. Although he was a tech sergeant at the time he wrote to Father Prokes, Antonic's engineering skills were superior enough to bring him up through the ranks of the Army. He qualified to become a warrant officer, an officer's rank that is achieved through technical skill rather than being commissioned. His placement as a warrant officer was a privilege that was limited to few in the military.

Antonic's gratitude for his upbringing by the priests and nuns of the Hessoun Home is obvious in his letter to Father Prokes.

He expressed his appreciation for the recognition all the former orphans, now serving their country, were getting in the church's *Messenger* bulletin.

> August 30, 1943
>
> Somewhere in the South West Pacific
>
> Dear Father Prokes,
>
> I don't know weather you know me or not but I'm Sergeant George Antonic a former orphan boy. Married orphan girl from there. Marie Stowyznski, I think a lot of the good sisters and thank them for all they did for me (and) all Mr. John Fabick, Sr. did. I was one of his employees since I left the orphanage which was about 11 years ago and he taught me and sent me to diesel schools and made a good man and a good diesel mechanic, which I think was the will of God because right now I'm giving all my strength and knowledge to our country in the US Army Engineers.
>
> Well Father the thing I'm writing mostly about is the Sunday missal which you have sent me that was really what I needed we have mass here about once a week and here in the jungle and come to think about it we are very lucky to have mass. Also thank you for The Messenger wish you would send me one every month. Also seen my name on the orphanage honor roll (thank you all for remembering us orphans). I also thank all the benefactors of the orphanage and the Home front, and hope they keep the good work up because we over here will do our part. I close for now, and may God bless you.
>
> Your orphan friend,
>
> Sgt. George Antonic

Antonic was not the only former Hessoun orphan to serve in the military during war. In all, twenty of the orphans fought as members of various branches, including several sets of brothers. These included Anthony and Frank Nekula and Arthur and John

Stawicynki, who served in the Army and Navy as well as the Vanicek siblings.

Private Joe Vanicek and his brothers were the sons of Czech immigrants. Their mother, Kathryn, owned and operated a bakery, but her death left the children with no home. The Hessoun Home took them in. When the war began, Brothers Frank and Joe went into the Army, while Bill joined the Navy. As the war in Europe was coming to an end, some of the bloodiest fighting was still happening in the Pacific. Fighting to take the Japanese island of Okinawa began in March 1945 and lasted for 82 days. Nearly 84,000 American and British soldiers and sailors lost their lives taking the island. Among them was 21-year-old Joe, who was killed on April 30. He is buried in Resurrection Cemetery in South St. Louis County.

One of the most interesting instances of service was that of Margaret Michalik. Upon coming of age, Margaret joined the US Marines. Her service took her to various stations across the country including time in Washington, DC. Two of her brothers, William and Frank, were also in the fight. At one point, Sergeant Margaret Michalik achieved the honor of selling the most war bonds during the 7th War Loan Drive and was cited personally for her efforts by USMC commandant and Medal of Honor recipient General Alexander Vandergrift.

Tragically, Margaret lost her brother, George, who was serving in the Navy in the Pacific in 1944. Seaman First Class George Michalik, US Navy, was buried at sea. His name is included on a tablet listing those buried at sea at the Manila American Cemetery in the Philippines.

In January 1945, Sergeant Margaret Michalik had the honor of attending President Roosevelt's fourth inaugural ball, then, after his sudden death the following April, she was chosen to march in the parade guard escorting the President's casket. Michalik wrote to Father Prokes a letter later printed in the *Messenger* about the experience. "Father," she wrote, "just a few months ago I wrote you that I attended the president's inaugural ball. Little did I think that so soon I would be escorting the president's body to his last resting place. I happen to be one of the lucky members of the military personnel to be appointed a member of the honorary parade. As his body passed, I said almost aloud, 'Good-bye Mr. President, and when you get up there look up my brother who just died in the Pacific."

When the war ended, Margaret returned to St. Louis and married George Antonic's brother, Steve, who completed his service as a master sergeant in an Army engineering unit. He passed away in 1963, Margaret in 2017. They are both buried in Jefferson Barracks National Cemetery.

After the war, George Antonic spent his life working as he had in the military, in the heavy equipment service. His obituary noted his membership in the International Union of Operating Engineers Local #573. Captain George A. Antonic passed away in 1997. He is buried next to his wife, Mary, in Jefferson Barracks National Cemetery.

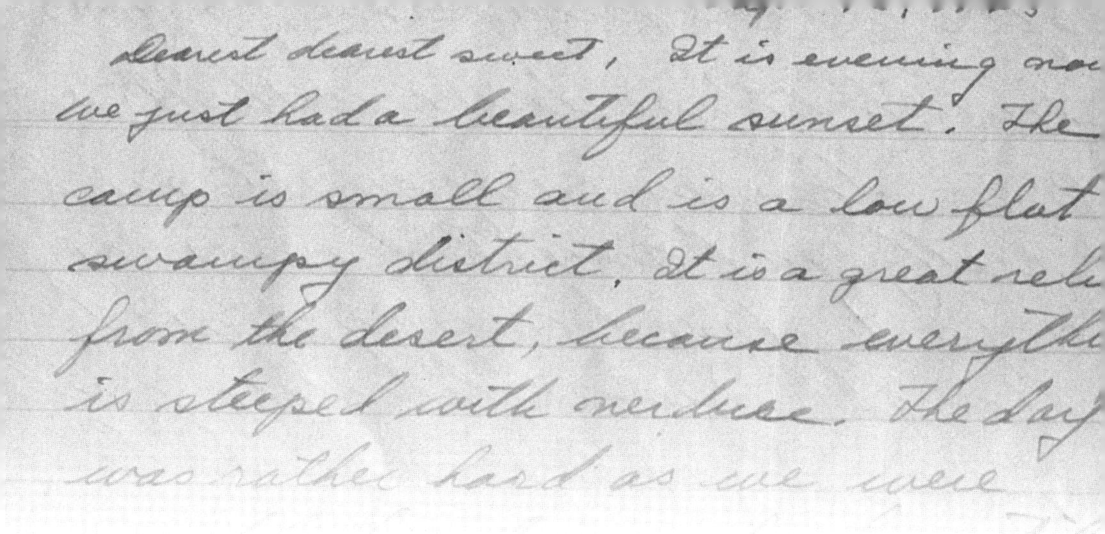
Dearest dearest sweet, It is evening no
we just had a beautiful sunset. The
camp is small and is a low flat
swampy district. It is a great rel
from the desert, because everyth
is steeped with verdure. The day
was rather hard as we were

Charles Waugh letter, September 12, 1943. *Collections of the Missouri Historical Society*

"I JUST CLOSED MY EYES AND THOUGHT I WAS DANCING WITH YOU." — CAPTAIN CHARLES WAUGH, US ARMY AIR CORPS

From an airfield in Hunan Province, China, an Army Air Force B-25 Mitchell bomber took off bound for the Pacific coast several hundred kilometers away. Its mission was to hit Japanese merchant ships off the Chinese coast as part of a campaign to disrupt the enemy supply lines that were reinforcing the occupying Japanese armies in China. To make the journey, American planes had to fly over Japanese occupied territory, which included all the Chinese coastal areas. It was a long and dangerous flight, as the Allied bases were located far inland, but the mission was successful, and the

This wedding photo of Charles and Ella Waugh was likely restaged just before Charles's departure overseas. Perhaps he requested this photo as a keepsake to take with him. He was not in the service when they married in 1940. *Collections of the Missouri Historical Society*

Mitchell turned around and headed back to its home base. Aboard this light, two-engine bomber was 40-year-old St. Louisan Charles Lincoln Waugh, an attorney turned military intelligence officer.

Charles Waugh grew up on Missouri Avenue just down the block from McKinley High School. His father, George Waugh, owned a mercantile store in the city. He and his wife, Mary, would have nine children together. Charles was the youngest. He attended Soldan High School before attending the University of Missouri. After returning home, he took night classes to get his law degree from Washington University.

As a young attorney, Charles was doing well. He secured a job with the city, becoming a city counselor and later a special tax attorney at City Hall. He was also a partner at a small firm with two other attorneys and a member of the Order of the Coif, an honorary legal society.

Somewhere along the way, Charles met Ella. She was a trained artist who had studied sculpture under the tutelage of noted Swedish sculptor Carl Milles at the Cranbrook Institute in Detroit. Milles is familiar to St. Louisans as the sculptor who created the landmark *Meeting of the Waters* fountain across from Union Station in downtown St. Louis. Ella also had spent time as a resident artist at the Pennsylvania Academy of Art. After returning to St. Louis, she worked as an art educator at the one-time St. Louis Children's Museum, among others.

The two were very much in love, and in December 1940, they were married in the parlor of her brother's home on Kingsbury Boulevard. Neither Charles nor Ella professed to be members of any faith, which is likely why they asked Judge William D. Becker to officiate their wedding rather than a member of the clergy. The judge and Charles were also friends, and when Becker announced his intentions to run for mayor of St. Louis in the upcoming municipal elections of 1941, Charles served as Becker's campaign secretary.

Charles and Ella took a home on Maryland Avenue and settled in to begin their lives together. Charles was helping with the Becker campaign. He was busy with his law firm and serving on civic boards. Ella was staying active in the arts community by presenting talks at the Wednesday Club and judging local art contests. The Waughs were living the lives of an up-and-coming St. Louis couple. But one year later, life would take a drastic turn.

Just a week shy of their first wedding anniversary, the war began. One can only guess as to the discussions that took place in the Waugh home between the couple, but Charles, who was already in his late 30s, made the decision to enlist in the Army Air Force. He did so in 1942.

Charles was first sent to Officer Training School in Miami. His educational and legal background seemed like a good fit for a position in military intelligence, so he was selected to attend the Air Intelligence School in Harrisburg, Pennsylvania. The program at AIC focused largely on analyzing intelligence photographs and training officers for aerial intelligence gathering. Once he had completed the training, he was assigned to become part of a new operation, the CBI.

The China-Burma-India Theater, as it was called, was one of the most complex of the war. Since the Japanese controlled the seas around China and much of the coastal areas, all supplies had to be flown into China from India. This herculean task was known as "Flying the Hump," the hump being the 15,000-foot peaks of the Himalayas. This crucial lifeline between British India and the remote wilderness of China began in 1942, when four civilian cargo DC-3s made the trip over the mountains carrying fuel bound for those bombers that had survived and made it to China after US Army Colonel Jimmy Doolittle's famous April 1942 bombing raid on Tokyo.

President Roosevelt had promised the Chinese that the Allies would provide them with the supplies and equipment they needed to defeat the Japanese in China, but besides overcoming the treacherous conditions of the Himalayas was an equally mountainous problem: the long-running civil war in China. China was a country deeply divided physically and politically. Nationalist Chinese forces under leader Chiang Kai-shek held regions in the south and central provinces, while Communist leader Mao Tse-tung held regions of the north. Both were at war with the occupying Japanese, but neither would cooperate with the other or consolidate their armies to drive out the enemy.

American commanders managed to negotiate with both sides and were able to build air bases in strategic locations across central China. Some airfields existed already, such as in Kunming where the noted American volunteer fighter pilots, the Flying Tigers, had a squadron.

At first the CBI outfit struggled to make even the most basic operations work. The Army had provided it with few planes and even fewer parts to maintain them. Often the work had to stop because the planes were grounded for maintenance. Furthermore, it was also difficult to build airstrips in the dense Burmese jungle. Adding to the difficulty was the continued advancement of Japanese troops in the early months of the war. In one instance, a daring pilot managed to evacuate 75 people from a rudimentary airfield in the Burmese city of Myitkyina just as Japanese troops were entering the outskirts. The story is made extraordinary because the old DC-3 he was flying was designed to carry no more than 28 passengers.

The primary goal of the CBI operations in those early days of the war was to keep the Burma Road up and running. Completed in 1939, the Burma Road served as a vital supply route, connecting the port of Rangoon (now Yangon) in Burma to Kunming in China's Yunnan province. This 717-mile road enabled the transportation of war goods to China. However, when Japanese forces captured Burma, they cut off the road at its source.

With the closure of the Burma Road, the US Army Air Force was forced to initiate the ambitious airlift operation. These missions presented significant challenges, including treacherous weather conditions, lack of reliable navigation aids, and the formidable terrain of the Himalayas. Despite these obstacles, the airlift continued daily until August 1945, delivering approximately 650,000 tons of material to China at great cost in men and aircraft. General Albert C. Wedemeyer, commander of US Forces in China, described "Flying the Hump" as "the foremost and by far the most dangerous, difficult, and historic achievement of the entire war."

Against the backdrop of the struggle in Asia was Charles and Ella's correspondence. The AAF sent him to India to undergo additional intelligence training and assist with the CBI operations there. They wrote frequently, and there's no doubt based on his letters that Charles wished to be home with her, but it is also clear that he was fascinated by the adventure he was undertaking. He related his experiences to Ella in vivid passages that described the sights, sounds, and tastes of India and later China. But one also senses the deep sense of loneliness and longing he experienced by being separated from his love by thousands of miles.

> Somewhere in India
>
> Sept 12, 1943
>
> Dearest, dearest, sweet, it is evening now. We just had a beautiful sunset! The camp is small and is a low flat swampy district. It is a great relief from the desert because

> everything is steeped with verdure. The day was rather hard as we were unable to get any food until evening, when we had a delicious meal.
>
> Last night I attended a dance at the Gymkhana (an English Club heavily patronized by American officers) and I saw Mrs. Betty Bathurst Brown, who is the wife of an English officer who is now at the front. I first met her at the dance at the intelligence school. She was with an English major and after much persuasion, I got him to let me dance with missus B-B. She was very sweet and pretty and smelled nice so I just closed my eyes and thought I was dancing with you. It made me real homesick for a while. A general here had a reception but I was not invited, but as I was on my way I stopped by the club and walked in and had the most delicious supper—prawn chow main, fried prawns, sandwiches of all kinds & appetizers and rice cookies. I ate all I could hold and then went home and to bed.

Just days later, Charles had flown "over the hump" and was now at his post in China. His next letter, written on September 16, 1943, is brimming with his desire to describe to her the details of his trip. He wrote:

> Dearest Onliest One, It is late afternoon and the Chinese red sun is slowly hiding itself behind green mountains which stretch ten thousand feet into the heavens. The sky is peaceful and clear with just a filegre of clouds. I am dead tired and longing for my bed which a Chinese boy is now making. Before long I will be sleeping, and dreaming about you.
>
> I wish I could write about a thrilling trip I had. It was positively fascinating and liltingly exciting. I will save it and tell it to you some night soon.

He went on to say that his first impressions of China were "delightful," and he found the Chinese people "sunny, willing, and friendly." Charles could not provide her with geographical specifics, but he described being near a "good sized city" in a location that was "very much like Denver, Colorado, and the climate most comfortable, cool, and delightful."

Then, in a letter dated October 9, 1943, he provided the details of a trip over the Himalayas as he had promised. He wrote,

> China
>
> October 9, 1943
>
> Saturday
>
> Dearest lover—
>
> The other day I had the most exciting time. I was awakened at about 5:00 in the morning and pulled out of bed and dressed, and then had breakfast. It was early morning and the sun was just coming over the mountains, and great billows of mist were rising in the valley. The heavy hum of the motors could be heard in the distance, and everyone was working hard at his job. We all went to the briefing room and heard the latest dope on the target and then grabbed our parachutes, guns and oxygen masks and we were driven to the ships—they were warm and anxious to get off. By this time the mist had thinned and the pilot took his position and the next Liberator (B24) rolled lumbering to the takeoff. Then, like a huge bird, it gracefully with motors roaring, rose in the blue sky above the yawning mountains. It was a thrilling experience for me as I was standing just behind the pilots and copilots seat, and had a beautiful view of the takeoff. Shortly after we rose into the air we met huge billowy white clouds and we had to rise to about 19,000 feet to fly above them. At this height we all had to put on our oxygen masks and go on oxygen. Soon we reached the Jap lines in the Burma China theater, I took a position as right waste gunner, and we open the Hatch and put the gun in position and scan the sky for enemy fighters. For over an hour we flew on instruments and were unable to see any land those earphones connected to the

ships speaker system and could hear all the inquiries and commands between the pilot and anxious crew members checking to see if everyone was in correct position and OK. After a while the navigator stated he could not find a checkpoint, and requested the pilot to go below the layer of clouds just beneath us. The pilot then took the plane to about 15,000 feet and for a while we flew between two layers of clouds, unable to see anything—with the high Himalayan somewhere below and around us, soon an opening came in the clouds and the navigator cited a river and gave the pilot a heading for the target. When we were about 10 miles away from the place where the navigator had estimated the target (A Chinese Jap held city) the skies cleared and we had a perfect run on the target, and soon the Bombardier called "bombs away" and these [illegible] yellow pills started their flight to earth. As it seemed to me that they would all fall way short of the target but as they fell they seemed to come over and all but one which fell a little over the target, hit it squarely we then turned and headed for a fueling point in India, and then returned to all base. No enemy planes were encountered, but it was extremely cold at this high altitude with the gun hatches open. While we were over *** territory I fired a few practice rounds on the gun, so now I classify myself, as an experienced waist gunner—but nobody else does.

This experience was very thrilling to me and gives me some idea of what the pilots and crews go through on a mission. It is a lot like the movies we have all seen. This most likely sounds very daring and dangerous to you, but actually it was a very tame affair to the crew who have made trips similar to this one often, and other missions in heavily defended *** areas with ack ack and Jap fighters filling the sky. The territory we went over had no anti aircraft, and although *** planes have been reported located in it from time to time, none actually have been encountered. It really is a lightly held *** outpost. Despite of the insignificance of the raid, it was very thrilling to me and I got to fly over and back the hump, which now gives me 3 trips—the mission took about 7 hours in the air.

I had hoped to get in town today for my mail but was unable to make it. I will try to get it tomorrow. Today was a very quiet day with no excitement. I tried to visit the Chinese town close by but could not even get transportation for it.

I am very well and hope you are the same. Played some volleyball with the fellas this afternoon. It is 11:00 and the light just went out. I love you sweetie. Charles

The mission described was typical of the bombing runs that the CBI mission undertook to destroy Japanese targets in Burma and China. In January 1944, US Army Air Force bomber groups were making frequent bombing raids on bridges, ports on the Yangtze River, and railroads in Burma. But Japanese fighters and bombers were also hitting back with bombing runs on the Allied bases. The situation was unnerving and hostile.

His next letter, written on January 8, 1944, spoke more of his personal views on the war and the opinions of others, including answering Ella's questions about the expressed opinions of another St. Louisan, General Leif Sverdrup, regarding interventionist ideology. Charles notes that his own opinions have changed and become more cynical, but he says he still believes the war is "not only inevitable but also necessary." And while he is "glad that he had a part in the fighting" he is ready for it to be over. He then reassures Ella that by all accounts, the war is soon to end.

China

8 Jan 1944

Saturday

Dearest Sweetheart,

It is just after lunch. The day is Gray and cold, and there is a heavy overcast in the sky. I am sitting in my room beside a charcoal fire rereading some of your letters which I have not previously answered in detail. You wrote that Edith was baking you a birthday cake—you lucky girl. And Speaking of your birthday, I found the note I started to write you on that important day. If you remember I was suddenly called away. That was the day May Fraley and his crew bailed out of the plane. I believe an account of the flight appeared in the Post-Dispatch. I do not know what date, as I did not see the article. I enclosed the note to let you know that I was thinking about you. You know that I would have liked to have been at home with you, and I still do. You wrote that Sverdrup is now less of an interventionist, and you ask me how I feel. In my present mood I am less of everything that should be worthwhile—less an interventionist, less a humanitarian, less a mixer. And yet in my heart and mind I am more convinced, that what happened was not only inevitable but also necessary. I am glad that I have had a part in the fighting, but I am ready to get out now. But don't misunderstand I do not have war nerves, I am not afraid and I know we are going to win. The truth is that I am too old just to love fighting, and I do not believe that but a handful are striving for the ultimate goal that made me as so enthusiastic—and that goes for both Americans and Chinese. Still one should realize that the mass cannot be better than its component parts I am not complaining about it, I am merely saying that, at last, I realize it and so do not want to exert further effort to change it. I had to quit the philosophical discourse to catch the 1:30 truck into town. At the last minute I decided to go in again to try to find a few things. The day turned worse and there was a fine drizzle all afternoon.

Take things easy, sweetie. The war will be over soon. At least, that is what all the reports I hear indicate. We all should give Russia a hand, she is doing a magnificent job. Not that I want to go there—God forbid—I want to come home and be with my pumpkin, and do nothing.

Love Charles

This was Charles's last letter. On January 26, 1944, his B-25 was returning from bombing the Japanese ports on the Chinese coast. As his Mitchell was coming in for a landing, the base was strafed by Japanese fighters. Charles's aircraft and the other Mitchells aborted their landing as the attack continued. As his plane was circling and waiting for the all clear to land, a violent thunderstorm appeared over the mountains. Caught in the violence of the storm, the bomber pitched and crashed. Charles was killed.

The St. Louis newspapers reported the death of the young city attorney. Ella's grief was pronounced. She attempted to learn all she could about the circumstances of the crash, including writing directly to Air Force General Hap Arnold, commander of the AAF. Arnold wrote her back and explained that he could not provide her with any further details, but he knew Charles as a fine officer and shared her sorrow.

Given the hardships of bringing home the remains of the fallen, Charles would be buried three times before coming home to his final resting place in the US Soldiers' and Airmen's Home National Cemetery in Washington, DC, in 1948. He was first buried with full religious rites (an article in the *Globe* noted that he was given Catholic, Protestant, and Jewish rites because he had written no preference on his military record) by chaplains at the American burial ground in Kunming, China, then reinterred in Hawaii until he could be moved to the US. This was typical in such cases.

Charles and Ella were both the unfortunate victims of circumstances far beyond their control, two people who were swept away from each other by the merciless tide of world events and a testament to the precariousness of our lives. Ella eventually moved on with her life. She continued to be active in the St. Louis art scene in the years to come. In 1958, she remarried and pursued a teaching career at Mary Institute and Columbia College in Columbia, Missouri. She passed away in 1984.

A final strange footnote in this story is found in the life of Mayor William Becker. Although not someone who served in the military, you could argue that Becker was a casualty of the war. Becker was by all accounts a close friend of Charles and Ella. He had officiated their wedding, and Charles had served on his 1941 mayoral campaign. Becker was an aviation enthusiast and supported strengthening St. Louis's position as a center of America's aeronautical industries.

On August 1, 1943, six months prior to Charles Waugh's deadly crash in China, Becker and nine other men stepped into a large glider at Lambert Field. The glider was a CG-4A built by Robertson Company and designed to carry men and materials used in airborne invasions. The glider was capable of carrying 13 airborne soldiers or heavier loads, such as one Jeep or 75 mm howitzer. Manufacturers around the country contracted to build the gliders, which were used extensively in D-Day, among other operations.

As a publicity demonstration of the glider's capabilities, Becker and other city officials were invited to take a test flight. The event attracted a large gathering of spectators on a Sunday afternoon. The demonstration began with a preflight demonstration of the glider flying with only its pilots. The flight had no issues, and the crowd watched it land smoothly and quietly.

The second flight was what the crowd was there to see. Mayor Becker entered the glider and was joined by Major William Robertson, builder of the glider and a pioneer of St. Louis's aviation industry. Lambert Field was Robertson's creation, as he had laid out the airport's runways and facilities just after World War I. He received the postal contract for St. Louis's first airmail service and employed a young Charles Lindbergh to fly the route from Lambert to Chicago. Also aboard was Thomas Dysart, the head of the city's Chamber of Commerce, a staunch advocate for St. Louis industry, and other Robertson and city representatives. The pilot, Captain Milton C. Klugh, had eight years of experience piloting gliders.

A day before the crash, a *Post-Dispatch* reporter questioned Mayor Becker about the safety of the flight and taking along so many city officials and guests. Becker explained he had total confidence in the safety of the flight, but added, "When our time comes to die, there isn't much we can do about it." It was a foreboding statement.

The next day, the crowd watched the C-47 tow plane pull the glider aloft. The twin-engine transport tow plane gained altitude and made two wide circles, taking the glider over the runway to give the spectators a clear view of the operation. Just before the third pass, the event's announcer informed the crowd that the glider would be released to land. They saw the cable release awkwardly, and then the glider's right wing began to rise at a 45-degree angle while the left wing moved downward. Pieces of the fuselage began to break away, and the glider plunged into a rapid nosedive. Within seconds, it was over as the glider smashed into the ground. Becker and all aboard were killed.

An investigation found that a faulty wing strut fitting that attached the wing to the fuselage had failed. The metal part was thin and broke under the weight and stress of the flight. It was the only known crash due to a faulty part. Nearly 10,000 of these models of gliders were manufactured during the war. They were used successfully for aerial landings in Sicily, Crete, and France.

On August 1, 1943, St. Louis Mayor William Becker was killed with nine other passengers aboard a demonstration flight of a military CG-4A military glider at Lambert Field. *Collections of the Missouri Historical Society*

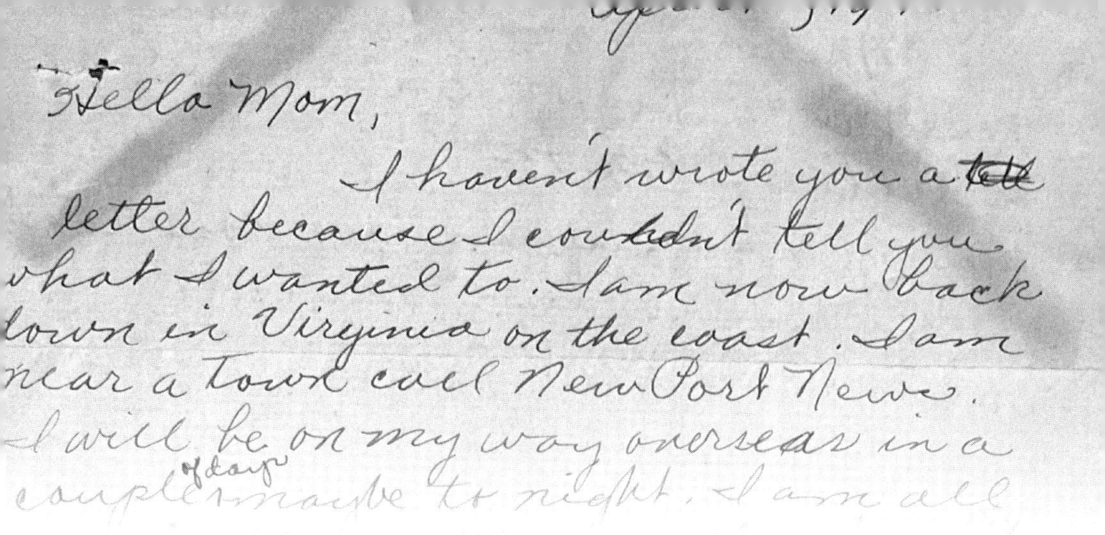

Hello Mom,

I haven't wrote you a letter because I couldn't tell you what I wanted to. I am now back down in Virginia on the coast. I am near a town call New Port News. I will be on my way overseas in a couple of days maybe to night. I am all

John E. Washington letter, April 10, 1944. *Collections of the Missouri Historical Society*

"SO MOTHER PLEASE DON'T WORRY."

— SERGEANT JOHN E. WASHINGTON, US ARMY

Leaving home for the first time is a big step in anyone's life. For many young men during World War II, leaving home for the first time meant going off to fight for their country. Such was the case for John E. Washington, age 18, of St. Louis, who entered the Army in 1943.

During his training and later service overseas, John wrote a series of letters to his mother, Rosetta, to reassure her that she should not worry about him while he was away. Of course, worrying about her son as he was thrust into conflict was inevitable, but John did his best to try to instill confidence in his well-being. In the following letter written just before he shipped out, his plea to his mother not to worry is repeated four times. Whether or not his mother gained some peace from this, we can only hope.

> April 10, 1944
>
> Dear Mom,
>
> I haven't wrote you a letter because I couldn't tell you what I wanted to. I am now back down in Virginia on the coast. I am near a town called New Port News. I will be on my way overseas in a couple of days, maybe tonight. I am all ready to go. Now Mother I don't want you to worry at all about me. There is no danger of getting over there at all. I wanted to tell you exactly what it is all about.
>
> Now don't worry. Promise me that you will write me often and I make it OK. Tell Marie I said hello & be a good girl. Tommie is here with me he is not going on the same boat that I am. In fact I'll be gone when he goes. You know Tommie (I bet). I don't need any money. I have made out another allotment you get $52.00 starting in May. Did Eula give you that jacket I sent to you? You are not supposed to know where I am or nothing, but I had to write a letter on the side.
>
> So Mother please don't worry. Don't write to me until you get a letter from me. You are not supposed to know that I am down here.
>
> With all my Love,
>
> Until we meet again. Don't worry please.
>
> I'll be alright.

John also kept a small diary which was dedicated less to his concerns about his mother and more to the concerns of his love back home, Belle. However, sadly for John, he was suffering from a heart ailment endemic in many soldiers, lost love. He dedicated quite a few lines to his thoughts on Belle even though it appears that his friends had informed him that Belle was no longer thinking about him. The news left him heartbroken. So far from home, it

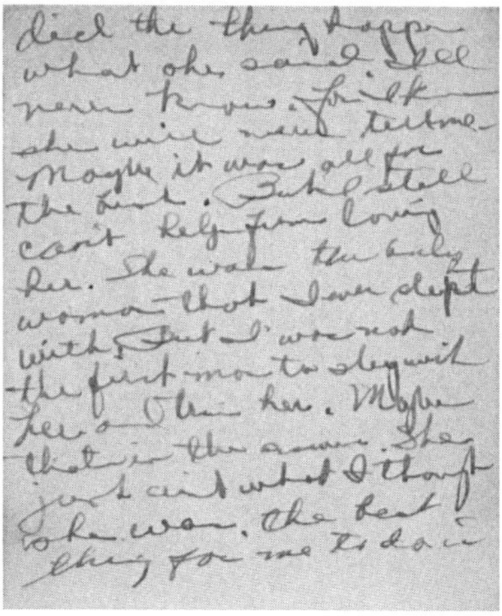

did the thing happen
what she said. Well
never knows. I think
she will never tell me.
Maybe it was all for
the best. But I still
can't help from loving
her. She was the only
woman that I ever slept
with. But I was not
the first man to sleep with
her [illegible] her. Maybe
that is the answer. She
just ain't what I thought
she was. The best
thing for me to do is

Pvt. Washington longed to see his sweetheart, Belle, back in St. Louis, but by all accounts, she seems to have moved on. *Collections of the Missouri Historical Society*

was a bad place to try to get over losing your first love.

John nevertheless did not seem to lose his sense of humor. At least, it appears he was trying to get on with his life and send some laughter home. In May 1944, he humorously explained the pleasures of Army life to his mother.

> 5/15/44
>
> Dear Mom,
>
> Sorry that I didn't write any sooner, but it's really not my fault. My buddie was to lazy to get his typewriter out of his bag, when he made up his mind he did it. Well honey I guess I'll tell you something about this army (my life). Well as I went to say Iy's really swell. A real clean healthy life. We are awakened each morning at the crack of each midnight. I can't see why they have reveille at five in the morning, everyone is asleep then. Sleep is the one thing I don't get much of. There is a guy on my right and night long he keeps asking questions that wouldn't be so darn bad except for the guy on my left all night long keeps answering him. (smile) But the thing that really awakens me is a good cold water shower this morning, for twenty minutes, why I like it so much I think that I will turn on the

water tomorrow morning. (smile) Dressing is the hardest. Something is always missing. Everybody takes anything, but there is a few guys who are very lucky they find things before people even lose them.

The food in camp is very good, they tell me. (smile) We have what they call or commonly known as religious cooks. Everything they make is either a sacrifice or a burnt offering. AS TO variety in food there is always a choice, take it or leave it. However the food is nutritious. For dinner today I had a plate of hash that contained 177 different vitamins and also three friendly germs. The cook told me that it was full of calories, and he was right, because I looked closely and I could see them walking around. And still my health continues to improve. When I came to the Army I weighed 150 pounds. When I weighed today I weighed 120 pounds. Tomorrow I intend to weigh without my full fill pack, over coat, and steel helmet on. (smile) Well it is mail call now, so I'll guess I'll close. Yesterday I received one letter that happens when you wont pay your friends. So long for now. Send my regards to all the family.

LOVE TO ALL.

S/Sgt John E. Washington

P.S. Got to hear mail call

When John arrived in Italy, he served with the 86th Quartermaster Railhead Company. The job of the men of the 86th was moving supplies to the front whether by rail or trucks. John in his diary made frequent references to "the dump" or supply dump as it was known. His military records list him as a clerk, so perhaps he was more on the inventory and tracking side of things, but it was not easy work, especially given his location close to the Italian front. He served in the Rome-Arno, North Apennines, and Po Valley campaigns. John received three bronze stars for his service.

When not working, he spent his downtime gambling and

thinking of Belle. Both left him without. "Feeling sort of sad or rather longing to be home. Lost about $60 dollars in the poker game. I try hard to keep from loving Belle for I know that I can not have her in the end. She has stopped all together," he wrote in October 1944.

John E. Washington's fortunes would turn upon his arrival back in the States. After leaving the Army, he spent some time in Chicago working before moving back home to St. Louis, where he found love, got married, and raised a family. Eventually, he became a minister and dedicated much of his life to helping those with addiction problems.

He passed away in 2007 at the age of 82. John is buried in Jefferson Barracks National Cemetery.

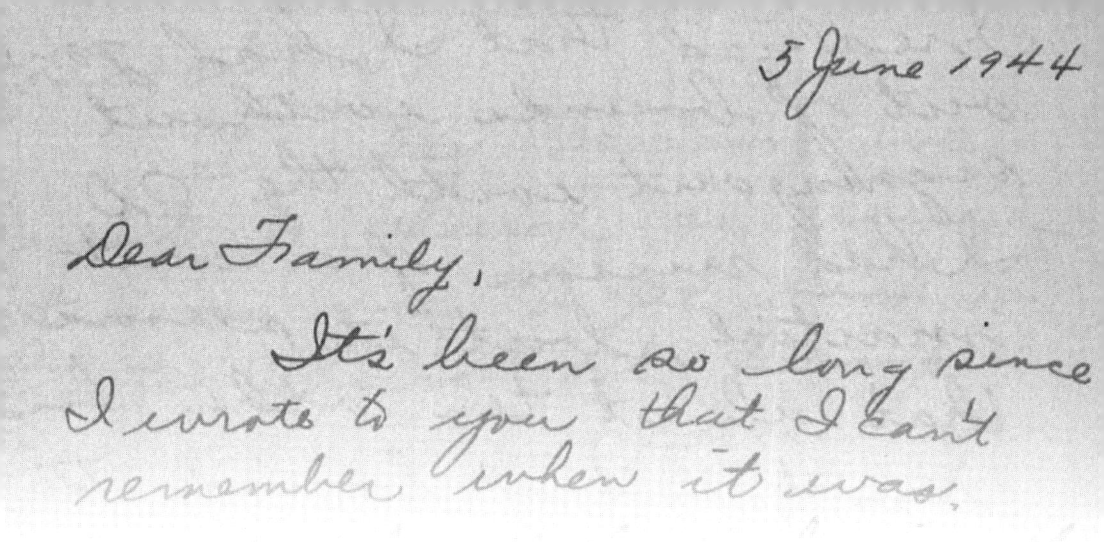

5 June 1944

Dear Family,

It's been so long since I wrote to you that I can't remember when it was.

Ensign Jean Schwarting letter, June 5, 1944. *The State Historical Society of Missouri*

"A LOT OF MOTHERS WOULD GET GRAY IF THEY COULD SEE THEIR DAUGHTERS FLYING AROUND HERE IN THE NAVY WAY."

— ENSIGN JEAN SCHWARTING, US NAVY

Wars are a catalyst for change. No society or nation emerges the same after it has endured the hardships and upheavals of an armed conflict. This is particularly true in terms of social change, and World War II is a prime example of the ways in which societies evolve by necessity. The need for women to enter the labor force to fill manufacturing jobs previously held by the men then away at war had a long-term effect on the presence of women in the workplace. Many people easily recognize Rosie the Riveter, the archetypal American female war production worker. The "Rosies" of World War II were seen as essential to keeping manufacturing running at full throttle while men were off fighting, but people generally believed that once the war was over, Rosies would return to their homes and kitchens. However, good-paying war work allowed many women a kind of financial independence that they had not experienced before while also providing a sense of unprecedented personal freedom outside the home. Society soon discovered that for a generation of young women it was hard to put the genie back in the bottle.

But it wasn't just war production that contributed to this new independence for American women. The military played its part too, most notably two new branches: the Women's Auxiliary Corps (WACS) of the United States Army and the Women Accepted for Volunteer Emergency Services (WAVES) of the US Naval Reserve. These two entities provided women with the opportunity to serve their country in positions that went beyond nursing and clerical work.

Women held support positions such as air traffic controllers, weather forecasters, mathematicians, gunnery instructors, and pharmacists. They packed parachutes and staffed naval hospitals. By the end of the war, more than 150,000 women were serving in the WACS and 86,000 women were serving in the WAVES in stations across the United States.

In St. Louis, the arrival of the first unit of WACS to Jefferson Barracks was met with fanfare at the base. The *Globe-Democrat* announced their arrival in March 1943 with the headline, "First Soldiers in Skirts Arrive for Duty at Jefferson Barracks." The women's unit consisted of "60 curled and powdered auxiliaries" freshly arrived from their training base in Des Moines. "Though the first contingent of Wacks arrived with fanfare, frivolity and the hope of possible romance on the part of more than one Jefferson Barracks soldier, they will soon begin serious and earnest work," stated the *Globe*.

The first platoon of the 152nd Post Headquarters Company was assigned to Jefferson Barracks to begin work as clerical support for the Army Air Corps's aeronautical mapping unit. A second unit of WACS consisting of "several hundred," noted the article, was soon to arrive to begin work driving trucks and assigned to technical work to relieve more men for combat.

Meanwhile, at a naval training school at Smith College in Massachusetts, a young St. Louis woman was beginning an exciting new chapter of her life as a WAVE. A newfound feeling of freedom and accomplishment is easily recognizable in the letters of Jean Madel Schwarting Anderson, who was accepted into the WAVES officer training program. At the time simply Jean Schwarting, she and her sister, June, were identical twins who attended Southwest High School. Their father, Harry, was an engineer for the American Car and Foundry Company in St. Louis. Jean attended Washington University and graduated in 1944 with a bachelor of science in business before joining the WAVES the same year.

Jean's letters to her parents are filled with stories of her travels around New England while attending the WAVES officers' training program in Northampton, Massachusetts. She and her fellow WAVES seemed to take every opportunity to venture around the region to explore towns and shops and visit attractions. Jean seemed particularly excited by the fact that being an officer gave her a certain degree of authority, including outranking some male members of the Navy.

WAVES received a vigorous daily regimen of physical and technical training to prepare them for Navy life. This included learning skills such as basic electrical maintenance that were considered outside the realm of most women. Such tasks are considered unexceptional undertakings today, but in Jean's youth, even the simplest technical skills and knowledge were not thought of as women's work. Writing to her parents, she noted that many of the things the young women were doing would turn their mothers' hair gray if they knew the extent of their training.

Despite the Navy's expectation that the women perform much of the same work as their male counterparts, those in command still felt that the WAVES should retain their feminine qualities. Consequently, the Navy brass declared that the WAVES's uniforms should be as fashionable as possible. New York couture fashion designer Mainbocher was contracted to create the women's uniforms, which consisted of three seasonal and dress versions: a seersucker with gray-and-white stripes, a dress white uniform, and dress blues. The shoes were Oxfords, which Jean must not have liked to wear when off duty because in one letter she wrote home asking for money to purchase new pumps for, as she noted, "morale purposes."

Jean received training in communications and would eventually be stationed in Washington, DC, where the greatest number of WAVES were posted. She worked as a code translator or "Code Girl." The work of Jean and other code workers like her greatly contributed to the effectiveness of military intelligence operations and strategic operations by passing along critical encoded communications from the Naval Security Station to naval operations around the world.

The following letter, written while Jean was still in training school, provides a true glimpse of her introduction to military life and the experiences of a young woman captivated by the freedoms and experiences that life in the modern Navy provided.

5 June 1944

Dear Family,

It's been so long since I wrote to you that I can't remember when it was.

With all the confusion of moving I've gotten terribly far behind in my letter writing.

This past weekend I stopped in Northhampton and messed around. Saturday afternoon I decided to go to South Hadley to have my picture taken by a man who treats the Waves very nice. I dressed up in a clean shirt and uniform and hopped on the bus. Since I couldn't go directly to South Hadley I went through Holyoke. I had a wonderful time riding around the country and it was Saturday night before I realized I had gone out of bounds without signing out with the O.D.

I had visions of a court martial but it seems that about ten other kids went out of bounds too and that it didn't matter.

Saturday night Delores Staggers and I went to the show. We saw "Snow White and the Seven Dwarfs" and "Bermuda Mystery." It was nice to see a movie and the show reminded me of the Roxy because we sat so long.

On the way home we stopped at Beckman's the local Busy Bee and Delores had a Diddle Daddle while I ate a banana split. These New Englanders really thin up ice cream concoctions.

Sunday morning we went to church as usual. It was nice to get back to Station Church at Hamp. Because we're officers now we get to sit up front with the Middies and Seamen in back of us. The saying up A.H.I.P (Rank has its privileges) is really true.

Sunday night we went to the show again to see "Shine on Harvest Moon." It was pretty good.

I'm on watch again for tonight and tomorrow. But this time it's as "Officer of the Day." Since we're moved to Capen the Battalion Commander decided the student officers should be O.D. as well as Mates. O.D. is very responsible position. The O.D. is directly under the Captain in the Chain of Command. I can tell lieutenants what to do here in Capen during the time I'm on duty, but I don't' think its advisable. But I do have complete power over the kids.

I'm excused from all classes tomorrow. Some of my duties

are to put all the kids to bed, get them up in the morning, and post the uniform of the day. I'll have to lock up Capen tonight and see that everything is secure.

Being on watch is one of the things that all officers do and is just part of the routine. Being O.D. here is a good training for when we go out in the field. Communications officers (WAVES) stand the same watches as men. Sometimes that means all-night duty with a gun too. More fun.

Wednesday is another exam. It seems that we're never finished with them.

It's nine o'clock now and its awfully pleasant being on duty. My desk is in the first living room and there's a fire crackling in the fireplace. It's been awfully cold here the last couple of days. I almost froze last night.

We have our seersuckers but its too cold to wear them. I hope its warm enough tomorrow to pipe the kids in seersuckers.

More trouble the Mate just called down to say there is a blown-out fuse on the deck. Luckily Miss Shepherd knew how to fix it.

We had so much fun in gym today. Since Capen is frame and part of a fire trap, Miss Shepherd decided we should try out all the fire escapes.

So during our gym period we hunted up every fire escape (ladders and ropes) and tested each one. You should have seen the kids who get dizzy when they're up in the air. They had quite a time climbing down a ladder. As one little girl said, "I can just see my mother sprouting a new gray hair if she could see me." A lot of mothers would get gray if they could see their daughters flying around here in the Navy way.

We played softball after we tested all the fire escapes. I slid into first base and cut a gash in my knee. But with a little self-applied first aid everything was fine.

Miss Shepherd went to bed and said that if there are any

more emergencies I should take care of them. Since its only half an hour until bed time not too much can happen.

I think I'll stop now. It's soon time to lock up. This cold weather makes me sleepy and its not going to be much fun to get up at five thirty.

Write soon.

Love,

Jean

Jean left the Navy in 1946 with the rank of lieutenant. She married soon after and moved to her new husband's hometown of Mexico, Missouri. They farmed and raised a family, but Jean did not remain at home. In 1959, she graduated with a master's degree in education from the University of Missouri. Thereafter, she taught third grade in the Mexico Public Schools until 1983.

Jean Schwarting Anderson passed away in 2019. She is buried in East Lawn Memorial Park in Mexico, Missouri.

WAVES were housed at Capen Hall on the Smith College campus in Northampton, Massachusetts. *The State Historical Society of Missouri*

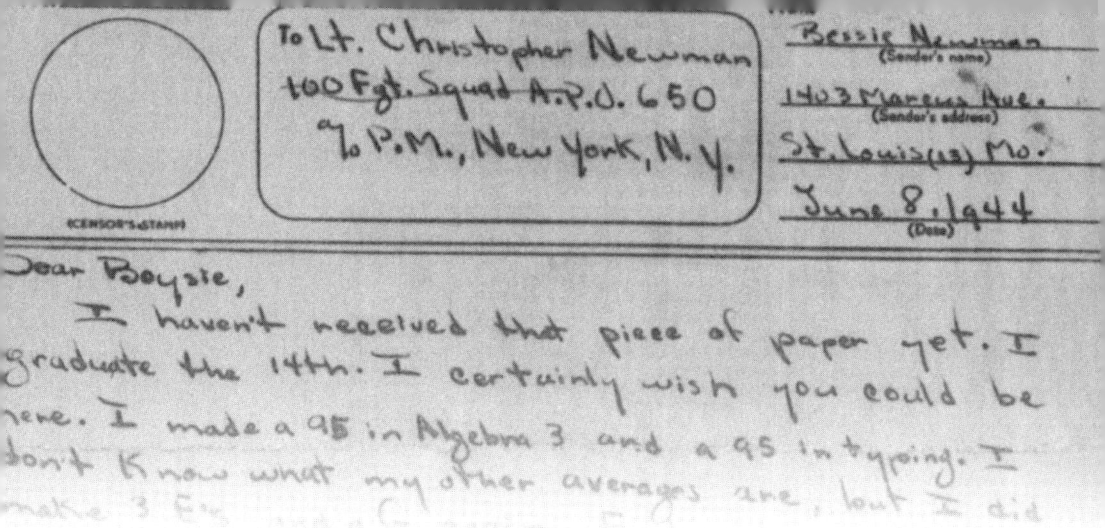
To Lt. Christopher Newman
100 Fgt. Squad A.P.O. 650
c/o P.M., New York, N.Y.

CENSOR'S STAMP

Bessie Newman
(Sender's name)
1403 Marcus Ave.
(Sender's address)
St. Louis (13) Mo.
June 8, 1944
(Date)

Dear Boysie,

I haven't received that piece of paper yet. I graduate the 14th. I certainly wish you could be here. I made a 95 in Algebra 3 and a 95 in typing. I don't know what my other averages are,

Bessie Newman V-mail, June 8, 1944. *Collections of the Missouri Historical Society*

BESSIE NEWMAN'S LETTER TO BIG BROTHER CAPTAIN CHRISTOPHER NEWMAN OF THE TUSKEGEE AIRMEN, US ARMY AIR FORCE

Few siblings in this country can brag that their brother served as a Tuskegee airman. Bessie Newman was one of those lucky few. Her brother, Lieutenant Christopher Newman, served as a member of the historic squadron that became the pride of black America.

Lieutenant Newman was yet another St. Louisan whose family had made the journey from Mississippi to Missouri in the Great Migration of the early 20th century. The family settled in the city's Mill Creek Valley neighborhood. Young Christopher attended

Vashon High School, and when he was 15 years old he stood among the crowds lining the streets of downtown St. Louis to see the aviator Charles Lindbergh pass by in a hero's parade. It was then and there that Newman decided that he too wanted to fly.

Newman took a job as an elevator operator to earn and save enough money to take flying lessons. It was an investment that paid

Tuskegee airmen, USAAF, gathered in front of a P-51 Mustang. *National Archives*

off. In October 1942, he enlisted in the Army Air Corps, which sent him to the famed Tuskegee Army Air Field to join other African American airmen in training. He was one of the few who proved their skill in the cockpit. "I put everything I had in it," he later said. Newman understood he was one of the privileged few and was determined to become a combat pilot. There were 72 flight trainees in his class when he began, but only 23 when it was over. His commission as second lieutenant was granted on October 1, 1943.

By the time Newman was ready for combat, the US had established bases in Italy. He and the others were members of the 100th Fighter Squadron, the famed Red Tails of the Tuskegee

Airmen. On February 4, 1944, Newman and his fellow airmen took off on their first mission flying Bell P-39 Airacobras. It was the first of 23 missions escorting US bombers to their targets. Newman returned home without a problem each time, but it was on his 24th mission that things took a bad turn. On his return to base, he was forced to crash land. The aircraft hit the ground and burst into flames. Newman was trapped inside while rescue crews worked to free him as the flames drew closer to the cockpit. As they pulled him, he managed to scramble onto the wing and to safety, but he was severely burned. The crash put him in the hospital for two months.

When Newman was cleared to fly again, the Red Tails had new planes, P-47 Thunderbolts. They flew these until the Army once again decided to change things up and provided them with P-51 Mustangs. Upon delivery of his Mustang, he christened it *Goodwiggle* after a popular dance move. It was while flying *Goodwiggle* that Newman had his second brush with death. Escorting a bombing run over Munich, Germany, Newman's plane received heavy flak damage. It was enough for him to abandon his plane and bail out. It wasn't just the plane that had been hit. Newman was bleeding as his parachute drifted down to the field below. Luckily, he was rescued six hours later. Two weeks later, Newman was back in the air.

Back in St. Louis, his friends and family followed all the news of the hometown hero. Bessie's letters allude to the many questions she received from everyone who knew of her brother. In one, she urged her brother to send a picture soon because "a lot of girls here want to see your picture." She was clearly proud of her brother.

V-Mail

TO: Lt. Christopher Newman
From: Bessie Newman
1403 Marcus Ave.
St. Louis (13) Mo.

June 8, 1944

Dear Boysie,

I haven't received that piece of paper yet. I graduate the 14th. I certainly wish you could be here. I made a 95 in algebra 3 and a 95 in typing. I don't know what my other averages are but I did make 3 E's and a G again. Earl is here and he looks funny without his glasses. Your picture is supposed to be in the Globe, a lady called today and asked mother about it and they sent a boy out here to get it. I saw the letter you wrote Mr. Evans and we're glad to know that you will only have a scar on your hand. Thanks for the money. Every time I go on Jefferson somebody says "Hey little Cris, How's Cris?" Last night I saw a man who has a very ugly scar on his neck, I know you know him. He asked me what happened to you and I told him so he said "Oh! I hope his pretty face doesn't get messed up." I said what pretty face?" He said "He has got a pretty face, he must have because he's your brother and anyway you look just like him." That made me feel very good. Miss Schunault Told me to tell you to be careful. She's so concerned about you. I'll try to get the picture for you. Aunt Bessie is here and she gave me $5.00.

Bessie

Newman received his captain's commission and completed 66 missions by the time the war ended. He returned to St. Louis and married Ernestine Perry. Newman remained in the reserves and owing to his skills as a combat pilot was recalled to duty in 1950 at the outbreak of the Korean War. During his time in Korea, he completed another 97 combat missions. He retired from the Air Force in 1952. For his service, he received the Purple Heart, the Distinguished Flying Cross, and an Air Medal with eight oak leaf clusters. In addition, each member of the Tuskegee Airmen received a replica of the Congressional Gold Medal in 2007 when President George W. Bush presented the Tuskegee Squadron with the honor.

Captain Christopher Newman died at the age of 100 in 2022. He is buried at Jefferson Barracks National Cemetery.

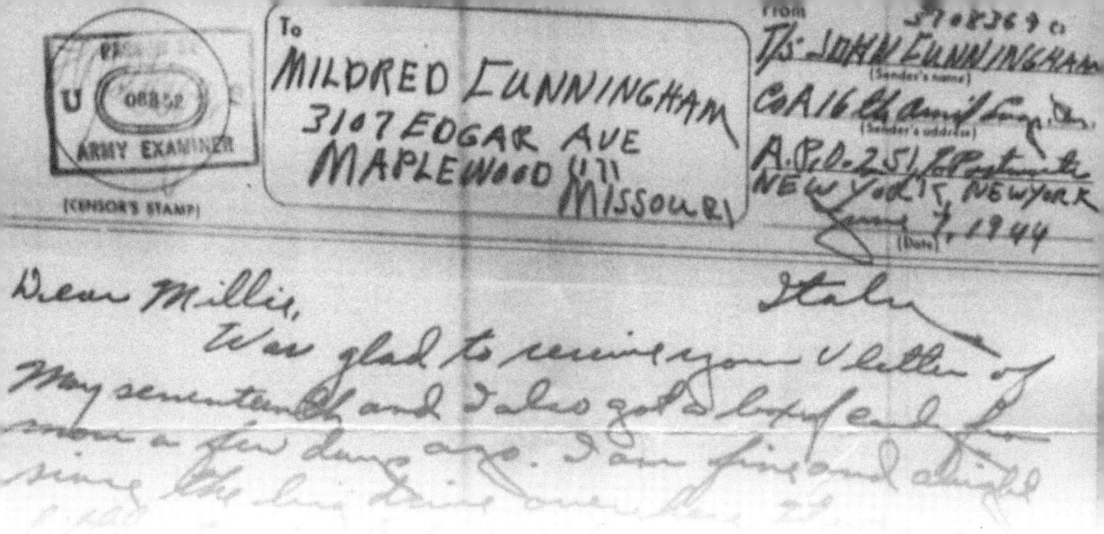

Tech Sgt. John Cunningham V-mail, June 7, 1944. *Collections of the Missouri Historical Society*

"OVERSEAS QUITE A LONG TIME NOW." — TECH SGT. JOHN CUNNINGHAM, US ARMY

The Cunninghams were a Montgomery County, Missouri, family. They lived a rural life in this east-central Missouri county that, like most prewar regions of the state, still relied mostly on agriculture for its livelihood. Frank Cunningham operated a feed and farm implement store in Montgomery City, where he and his wife, Katherine, shared a home with their five children and two of his sisters.

When their youngest daughter, Mildred, or Millie as she was called, graduated from high school, she moved to St. Louis and took a job with one of the city's largest department stores, Stix, Baer, & Fuller. Millie's older brother, John, worked at the family feed store. The two, who were the closest in ages of the Cunningham children, maintained a close connection. During the war, Millie kept a close correspondence with John, a soldier in the 16th Armored Engineers Battalion of the First Armored Division.

Twenty-four-year-old John had married a woman named Mary shortly prior to his enlistment in the Army, but judging by his letters to Millie, his wife was not a reliable letter writer and he rarely heard from her. Luckily, Millie kept John's lifelines connected to the folks back home.

The two siblings wrote to each other as often as they could. John told her it wasn't always easy for him to find the time, and with good reason. The 16th Armored Engineers were a busy bunch. The men of the 16th were some of the first to see combat once American forces began to actively engage in offensive operations in the European theater.

John enlisted in the Army in 1942 and was sent to Fort Knox, Kentucky, where the 16th trained. There the men learned to operate the heavy machinery whose task was to clear whatever obstacles lay in their way so the men, equipment, and vehicles of the First Armored Division could push forward.

In 1942, Morocco and Algeria were under the control of Vichy France, the pro-German government that maintained a degree of independence after Hitler's invasion of France in 1940. East of these two countries the Italians and Germans held Tunisia and Libya. North Africa was firmly in the hands of the Axis powers, and the only check on their total domination of the Middle East was Britain's military cooperation with Egypt.

Throughout 1941 and early 1942, the British attempted to cut off the Axis supply lines to Europe, but they struggled to maintain any ground they had captured from the Germans and Italians. Finally, late in 1942, enough American forces had gathered in England to launch an invasion of North Africa. The entire operation was fraught with uncertainty since American soldiers were inexperienced and untested in battle; sending large amounts of men and equipment by sea was risky in the U-boat-infested waters of the Atlantic, and no one knew how determined the French troops in Morocco and Algeria might be toward fighting to retrain control of the region.

In November 1942, Operation Torch got underway. Private John Cunningham's 16th Armored Engineers were included in the Center Task Forces whose object was to land around the Algerian port city of Oran. The landing was difficult due to the shallow water and sandbars along the coast, but once the troops landed, they met with no resistance. The landing may have been easy, but the push inland would not be. Cunningham's division was responsible for creating roadblocks to slow the advance of German and Italian tanks and vehicles or demolishing the roads altogether. They cleared the thousands of land mines laid by the Germans throughout the desert plains. After battles the men of the 16th cleared away the destroyed tanks, trucks, and other vehicles littering the roads. On other occasions they were ordered to build new roads. It was hard work in the unforgiving heat of the African deserts.

Seven months of attacks and counterattacks ensued until finally in May 1943, Allied forces surrounded the remaining 250,000 exhausted German and Italians troops and took them prisoner. The Allies could now turn their attention to the invasion of Italy.

There was a lull in the fighting long enough for John to send off a few lines to Millie on May 3, 1944. In this letter, he mentioned receiving a letter informing him that a fellow Montgomery Countian named Jim Marlow was missing. Marlow, a sailor and perhaps a childhood friend of John's, was never found. Today, there is a stone in the Montgomery City Cemetery that reads, "James E. Marlow, US Navy, missing in action, March 28, 1944."

Marlow's MIA status and the deaths of several of John's family members since he had been away fighting left him to ponder his own good fortune. He told Millie, "When I get to thinking about [it] I guess I have been mighty lucky and should thank my lucky stars. Also about Grandma passing, gee I can hardly believe that so many of my relatives have gone since I am where there are air raids, shells flying, and all that kind of stuff and I am still planning on making it back to the states."

Staying alive was a difficult maneuver in Italy. Fighting their way through the Italian campaign from Sicily to Rome and northward was a tough, bloody journey that took the lives of thousands of Allied troops. The infantry and artillery divisions fought mile by mile, but they often got where they were going because of the advanced work performed by combat engineers like John. He and his company had the unenviable job of clearing mines, removing destroyed equipment, and building roads and bridges while they were also fighting. But they were still advancing mile by mile.

By June 1944, the Allied forces had reached the outskirts of Rome. The Germans pulled back, and the city fell to the Americans on June 5, a day before the launch of Operation Overlord or D-Day, in France. John wrote Millie to tell her that he had seen the eternal city along with a few words hinting at the rough time they had driving the Germans back. You get a hint of pride from his story of seeing the cheering Romans lining the streets to greet the parading American troops.

T/5 John Cunningham

June 7, 1944

Dear Millie,

Was glad to receive your V letter of May seventeen and I also got a box of candy from mom a few days ago. I am fine and alright since the big drive over here. It was a little tough at first but now believe we have the krauts on the run. I saw Rome and it is a beautiful city. It is much cleaner and nicer than any of the cities in southern Italy. The people look to be a better class and dressed better. They lined the streets and cheered as we passed thru that was a great day for all of us for we have been fighting so long to get here. Heard the news of the invasion and that sounds good. I really ought to make it home soon now. At least every one morale has sure gone up the last few days. Hope you are well and don't work to hard. It has been nice here lately. I am all tan. When I get a chance will tell you of what I have seen lately. Write soon.

Love,

John

With the news of D-Day, focus on the European Theater shifted to the French invasion, but the men on the ground in Italy kept driving hard against the Germans. After pulling out of Rome, the Germans had regrouped and formed the Gothic Line in Northern Italy. They were dug in deep and fighting aggressively to maintain a foothold.

A month after Rome had been liberated, the push toward Florence was raging, and casualties were high. In his last letter to Millie, her brother praised her for the USO work she had told him about in a previous letter. He took a line to kid her about American soldiers getting too much special treatment back in the states before they were deployed. It was a bittersweet remark, when he said that he was nevertheless glad to see "someone enjoying life" just as he lamented, "All I am doing is sweating this getting home alive and in one piece."

John was clearly doing his part, but his final letter bears the signs of battle fatigue. He wrote Millie on June 29, 1944.

V-Mail
T/5 John Cunningham
TO Miss Mildred Cunningham
3107 Edgar Ave
Maplewood, Missouri

June 29, 1944

Dear Millie,

I was glad to receive your letters of June fifteen. I also had one from Ernest Werner written the seventeenth and said he was going to St. Louis that day and would see or call you so perhaps he seen you I hope.

Millie where is Camp Pendleton located. So many new one's sprung up after I left I don't know where a lot are located.

Well you people sure seem to take good care of the soldiers back home. Wish we could enjoy some of those good times. Am afraid that you spoil those boys before you send them over. Oh well glad to see someone enjoying life. I know I will when I get the chance. All I am doing is sweating this getting home alive and in one piece. So you better keep praying for we will need it. All my writing is done on the run so don't expect to many from me. As long as it ends the war sooner [illegible] and everything sounds good and is going that way so I will be seeing you [illegible]

Write soon. Don't try to do too much. Love, John

Seven days later, John was killed in combat fighting somewhere in northern Italy.

In 1949, Charles Frank Cunningham made the arrangements to bring his son, John, home for burial in Montgomery City. John rests in St. Mary's Cemetery.

There was one last letter from Millie to John written, unbeknownst to her, two days after his death. She ended the letter by expressing hope that he would soon get his furlough and be home for Christmas, but like so many others there was not to be another Christmas with the family.

Millie would never forget her brother. She eventually met and married a World War II serviceman, PFC Jefferson John Patrick Kelly, US Army Air Force, and they lived a long life together. Jefferson and Millie are buried next to each other in Jefferson Barracks National Cemetery.

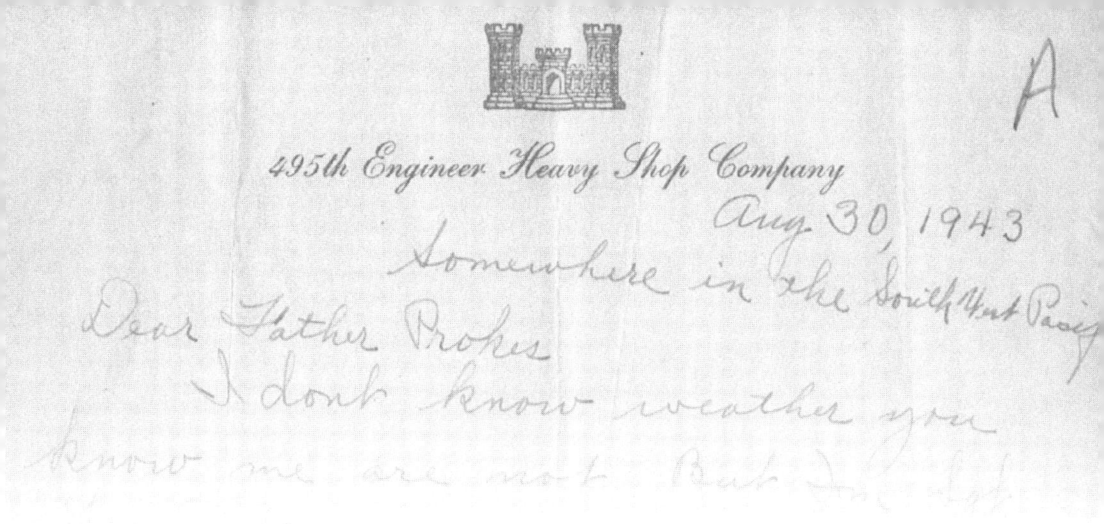
A

495th Engineer Heavy Shop Company

Aug. 30, 1943

Somewhere in the South West Pacif

Dear Father Prokes

I don't know weather you

know me are not. But I

John J. Mika letter, September 11, 1944. *St. Louis County Parks and Recreation*

"I'VE SEEN A LITTLE ACTION." — PRIVATE JOHN J. MIKA, US ARMY

Fear of an impending attack on America worried President Roosevelt and military commanders in Washington months before the bombing of Pearl Harbor. Concerns for such an attack focused largely on Germany, not Japan, as the potential belligerent, so cities along the Eastern Seaboard were considered particularly vulnerable. Newsreel footage of the devastation of the London Blitz and the bombing of Soviet cities after the German invasion of Russia deepened those fears. The Roosevelt administration's answer was to create the Office of Civil Defense (OCD), an agency that would coordinate state and federal preparedness strategies across the country.

After the outbreak of the war, the OCD became very visible and active in preparing plans of action in the event of air raids and other attacks. St. Louis, like most major American cities, would train an army of civilian civil defense wardens whose job it was to coordinate local responses. It was a job that those who were chosen to serve took very seriously. People of all ages and backgrounds could participate, and one of the most active groups was the hundreds of Catholic nuns in St. Louis.

Sister Antoine Mika of the School Sisters of Notre Dame was one of 535 nuns from 52 different orders and 152 St. Louis Catholic institutions who graduated from the air raid warden training program in August 1942. Earlier that spring, an initial 19 sisters had finished the program, paving the way for hundreds more, including Sister Antoine, to enroll in the program. Most of the sisters were teachers or nurses and responsible only for supervising the activities within the institutions where they were residents, but they were logical choices for the civil defense roles.

The graduation ceremony was attended by St. Louis Mayor William Becker and Cardinal John Joseph Glennon of the Archdiocese. Becker addressed the sisters and told them that they should always be alert and mindful that the Axis powers did not respect their religion. It was their duty to be aware of potential sabotage as well as the threat of air raids. Cardinal Glennon reminded them that their service was an essential factor in keeping up public morale.

Luckily, neither Sister Antoine nor any of the nuns ever had to deal with a crisis in the city, but she still had her worries. John J. Mika was Sister Antoine's brother. He was an Army private fighting in France. Sister Antoine, whose given name was Evelyn Mika, and John grew up together in Fort Madison, Iowa, before she left to take the orders in St. Louis in the 1930s. Evelyn professed her first vows in 1936 and final vows in 1942 to become Sister Antoine.

In the following letter written in September 1944, John informed her that he had seen some combat and witnessed aircraft shot down, but as always he could not tell her more.

V-Mail
Pvt. John J. Mika
Sept 11, 1944
TO: Sister M. Antoine
9605 W. Milton St.
Overland, Missouri USA

Dear Sister,

I received your very nice letter today and was glad to hear from you. How are you and the rest of the nuns down there? OK, I hope. I'm still the same as always. I'm glad you had a nice summer up north. Lets hope you can go again next summer. Thanks a million for remembering Wilma and I on our wedding day. I write to mother as often as I can. She probably told you that I was in France now. I served Mass twice in France and once in England. So it looks like I still get a little practice at serving. I've seen a little action and planes shot down so far. That is about all I can tell you now. Maybe someday I can sit down to tell you some things. How about it? I'll have to ring off for now and get to bed. So long for now. Love your brother,

Johnny

Civil defense wardens like Sister Antoine were issued air raid helmets and armbands to designate their positions. Their duties included educating their neighbors about civil defense procedures in case of attacks and air raids. First aid kits, flashlights, gas masks, whistles, and other response needs were standard-issue to most air wardens. Cities and towns were divided into sectors with each air warden covering a designated area.

In February 1942, the *Webster Groves News-Times* reported that there would eventually be 600 air wardens assigned to the town. It gives one a sense of the enormity of the endeavor. In total, some 50,000 wardens were commissioned in St. Louis City and County. Selecting and training OCD wardens was a full-time operation that included instruction on how to put out fires caused by incendiary bombs. Training manuals were issued by the OCD, but corporate sponsors were eager to get on the home front bandwagon and often provided them as branded handouts to the public.

First and foremost, the job of the air warden was to enforce city-imposed blackouts. The first blackout laws were set in place just after Pearl Harbor. All homes and businesses were to turn off lights and cover any lights that could not be extinguished, such as fire escape access lights. Large picture windows downtown such as those on the Missouri Athletics Club building were painted black to block out the interior lights. Not obeying the law could get you in real trouble. In 1943, John Jablonski parked his car in the middle of the street with its lights on during a blackout. He was approached by an African American air warden who told him to turn off his lights. Jablonski refused the order, including moving his car from the street. He was arrested and sent to court. At his trail, he declared that he was being tried by a kangaroo court and he was "no Nazi" but his declarations fell on deaf ears. The judge sentenced him to 10 days in the city workhouse.

Another violation was committed by Julia Loftus of North 15th Street. She had refused orders from the air warden to turn out the lights in the front and on the sides of her home, saying they were necessary. The court disagreed. She also received 10 days in the workhouse.

The blackouts continued through the end of the war. Although living under the blackout rules were necessary in such times, they were not particularly comforting. The bleak darkness of the city was a constant reminder of the presence of the war and enemy threat. It was no surprise then that when Victory in Europe or V-E Day was declared occurred in May 1945, the city celebrated by turning on all the lights.

Sister Antoine's service to St. Louis went way beyond her time as a civil defense warden. After earning a bachelor's degree in fine arts from Mount Mary College in Milwaukee, she finished two master's degrees from St. Louis University and the University of Notre Dame, respectively. Sister Antoine spent 54 years in education teaching at schools across the St. Louis area as well as in Illinois, Louisiana, Mississippi, and Texas. Sister Antoine Mika passed away in 2012 at the age of 94. She rests at the School Sisters of Notre Dame Motherhouse Cemetery in Lemay, Missouri.

Tech 5 John J. Mika returned to Fort Madison after the war. He passed in 1994 and is buried in Oakland Cemetery in Fort Madison, Iowa.

Alpen Brau Civil Defense Manual. *Collections of the Missouri Historical Society*

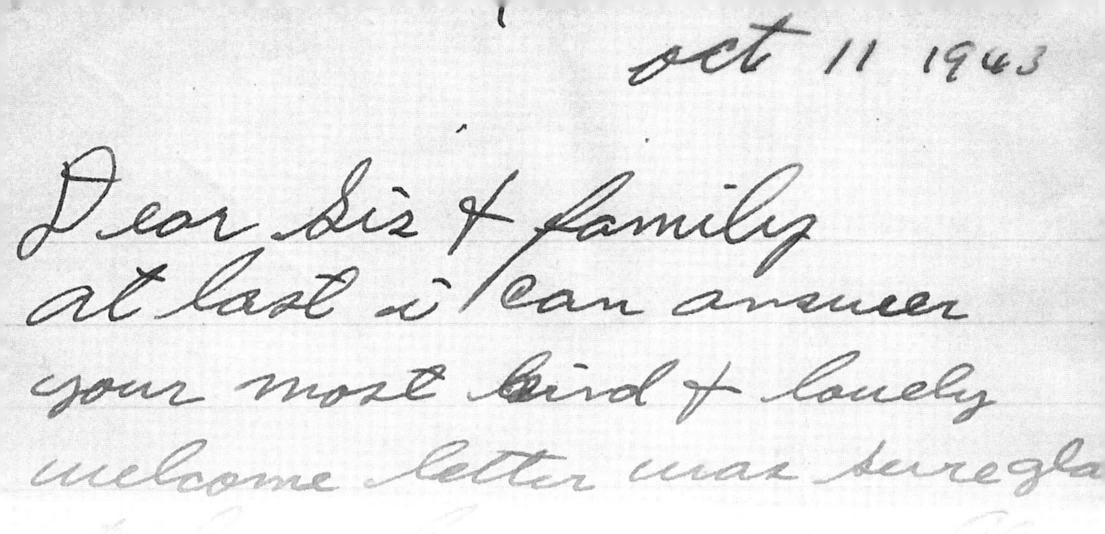
oct 11 1943

Dear Sis + family
at last i can answer
your most kind + lovely
welcome letter was sure gla

Private William Phillips letter, October 11, 1943. *St. Louis County Parks and Recreation*

"THE MINUTE I BECOME A CIVILIAN AGAIN I AM GOING TO BE A DIFFERENT PERSON."
— PRIVATE WILLIAM C. PHILLIPS, US ARMY

A month and a half after the Invasion of Normandy on D-Day, officially known as Operation Overlord, Allied troops were steadily pushing the Germans farther and farther inland from the English Channel. In the final weeks of July, the *Globe-Democrat* printed an account of traveling with General Eisenhower's soldiers by Associated Press reporter Robert Bunnelle, who described witnessing massive amounts of secured munitions and supplies offloaded by Allied troops lining the roads leading to Paris. Bunnelle expressed confidence that the Germans' swift retreat and failed attempts to keep the region within their control was a sign that victory for the Allies was a foregone conclusion. However, "there still must be hard and bloody fighting to achieve it," he warned for those who might think that the road ahead was an easy one. "Fighting was bitter, and casualties were high where our troops were actually engaged," he reported. In the days and weeks following the Allied push forward, news of St. Louisans who fell in that fighting as soldiers fought village to village began to appear in the city's newspapers.

Somewhere along the progressing front line was Private William C. Phillips, an infantryman from St. Louis's Downtown neighborhood. Bill, as he called himself, and his wife, Lena, shared an apartment on Fourth Street in the block directly behind today's Field House Museum. It was not far from where he lived, growing up in a working-class family of six. Bill's parents had reached their senior years by the time Bill was in his late teens, so he and his older siblings worked to support the family. These were the years of the Great Depression, and life was hard for most workers as they struggled from day to day, and high unemployment kept them on the breadline. But, according to the 1930 Federal Census, all the Phillips children were luckily employed in factory jobs. For his part, Bill worked for a railroad car manufacturer. It was a good job to have during those lean times, and 10 years later, Bill still listed it as his employer on the 1940 census.

Bill was drafted in 1943 and sent to Camp Gruber, Oklahoma, for basic training. Camp Gruber, located on 109 square miles of land near Muskogee, was one of the many new small bases constructed by the War Department across America between 1942 and 1943 to train the hundreds of thousands of soldiers needed to fight. If a St. Louisan found themselves in the Army, their first taste of Army life was usually experienced at either Camp Gruber or Fort Leonard Wood near Rolla.

Now Private Bill Phillips, he did not particularly adapt well to life in the military, but he still felt it was his duty despite his discomfort. He wrote to his sister from camp:

> Oct 11 1943
>
> Dear Sis & family
>
> At last I can answer your most kind & lovely welcome letter. Was sure glad to hear from one & all. These few lines leaves me OK today & hoping every body is the same up there. For the past 2 weeks we have been working Sunday & every day.
>
> Boy I sure wish this thing was over. The army is not for me but I got to take it any how.
>
> Well sis about all I can say is just keep the ball rolling the best you can.
>
> Bill

The following year, Private Phillips was in France with the 314th Infantry along with the rest of the Allied invasion forces doing their best to push the Germans farther toward the Fatherland. By his letter, we can assume that he had seen his fair share of the fighting. The Allies had killed nearly 6,000 German soldiers since landing at Normandy 23 days before his letter to his parents was written on June 29, 1944. An additional 37,000 German prisoners were taken, and the fighting near Caen in the northern coastal area continued to be a raging battle to dislodge the Wehrmacht from its entrenched positions.

One can sense the anxiety and longing for home and safety in Private Phillips's words home; it was a grueling set of circumstances for any soldier to be at the front. What he had witnessed and experienced also seems to have encouraged him to do some self-reflection and instill a new course in his life. Perhaps the death and destruction he witnessed made him realize the fragility and precariousness of life.

June 29, 1944

France

Dear mother, father, sister & brother & all

Just received your letter the other day & was sure glad to hear from you all. Folks for god sake don't wait for me to write because I don't know from one day to the other. I don't know where I will be, in fact, the letter I got from you Sis is the first one I got in two weeks, because when them darn dutchmen make a move we are just behind them with our steele ready to push in the pants & believe me they sure can run haha. Oh yes tell dad that I have all ready for got the count on what I promised, the dirty rats sure can beg for mercy for what we are doing.

Sis & all the rest of the home folks, believe me on one thing, the minute I become a civilian again I am going to be a different person & I don't mean maybe either. I am sure glad that mom got her pension check & hope dads get raised to match it. They both need all they can get.

Will close for this time as ever, Bill

To all my home folks

Love to one & all

Answer soon,

Hugs & kisses

The Americans were fighting mile by mile, a situation that the Allied planners had not anticipated. Eisenhower and the others had hoped for a faster push through France after the invasion, but the Germans pushed back harder than expected. Allied troops were advancing but at a much slower pace. Much of it could be attributed to the marshy conditions in northern France, the continuing presence of bad weather, and the obstructive tactics of the retreating Germans. In many villages along the German escape routes, they left behind snipers to slow and harass their pursuers.

The details are not known, but it was somewhere along this front, possibly near Saint-Lô, that Private Phillips became another casualty of the war. Sadly, his parents would receive the notice that all families feared: Bill was killed on July 21, 1944, somewhere in France. Bill's father sought more answers and wrote to Bill's commanding officers for details, but information of that kind was restricted by the War Department. Instead, he received the following letter from the chaplain of the 314th Infantry.

> Sept. 25, 1944
>
> Mr. James T. Phillips
> 2327 S. 3rd St
> St. Louis, Mo
>
> Dear Sir.
>
> Now that you have been officially notified, by the war department, of your son's death, I can answer your letter of last month.
>
> I want to express to you my deepest sympathy at your loss. Unfortunately, we are greatly restricted by the war department in what we can write directly to you. So I'm sending this note to let you know that a letter will follow, through channels, which will answer most of your questions. If after you receive the letter, I can be of any further assistance, please write me.
>
> With heartfelt sympathy, I remain
>
> Yours very truly,
>
> Jerome J. Sealy
>
> Chaplain 314th Inf.

Whether James Phillips received the answers he sought concerning his son's death, we cannot say. The aforementioned letter is not present in the archives at Jefferson Barrack Park. We do know that the 314th Infantry was pivotal in driving the Germans out of Cherbourg and paving the way for General Bradley to take Saint-Lô, a decisive victory for the Americans to drive the Germans out of France.

Private William C. Phillips's death not only deprived the Williams family of their son and brother, but wife Lena became a young widow. It was a situation that was too often suffered in cities and towns across America.

Bill was returned home to St. Louis for burial in the years following the war.

He is buried in Jefferson Barracks National Cemetery.

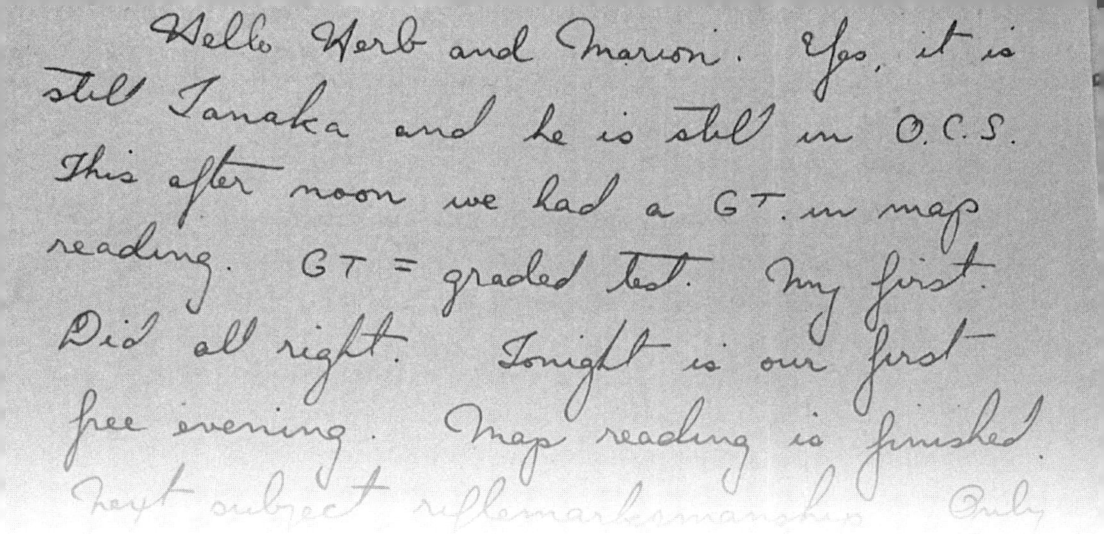
Hello Herb and Marion. Yes, it is still Tanaka and he is still in O.C.S. This after noon we had a G.T. in map reading. GT = graded test. My first. Did all right. Tonight is our first free evening. Map reading is finished. Next subject riflemarksmanship. Only

Joe K. Tanaka letter, October 4, 1944. *The State Historical Society of Missouri*

"THE TANAKA BOYS ARE TAKING OVER." – JOE KENICHIRO TANAKA, US ARMY

After the news of the bombing of Pearl Harbor by the Imperial Japanese Navy reached the mainland, few Americans were as fearful of what might lie ahead as those of Japanese descendent. Hatred and fear of all things associated with Japan manifested itself quickly in many parts of the US, and Japanese American families became vulnerable to those seeking an easy target and scapegoats. In St. Louis, far from the large Japanese communities on the West Coast, only four Japanese families lived in the city. Among those families were the Tanakas, led by father Haru and his wife, Gin. The couple had three sons: Joseph, Chester, and Edward, all three American born. The family operated a restaurant, the Tokyo Restaurant.

Joseph, the eldest brother, entered Washington University in the mid-1930s and graduated in 1938. After spending some time in New York City studying industrial design as a graduate student at Columbia University, he returned home and established a design firm.

On Sunday, December 7, 1941, Joe was attending the St. Louis Symphony when suddenly the concert was interrupted by an announcement that the Japanese had declared war on the US. The news left him and his family in shock. Joe's brother, Chester, explained years later in an oral history that he recalled being stunned by the news and confused as to why a small country with no sustainable resources would take on the powerful United States.

Fortunately for the Tanakas, they did not fall under immediate suspicion like the Japanese tourism representative Tetsu Uyeda. Rather, the Tanakas' situation was met with sympathy, according to Joe Tanaka. Many of his classmates were from families of German descent who recalled the anti-German sentiments that arose during World War I. They knew that the Tanakas had no more control over what was happening in Japan than had the German families of St. Louis over the leaders of Germany.

Like all young men, he was required to register for the Selective Service, and he was drafted. Joe sought to register as a conscientious objector, but the draft board ignored his request. Unlike the sympathy he experienced in his own neighborhood, the draft boards displayed more overt anti-Japanese attitudes, which he believed explained their denial of his objector status. Likewise, when his brother, Chester, voluntarily enlisted in the Army, he too ran up against prejudices within the draft board. When Chester sat down to be interviewed by the board prior to his service, the interviewer asked him what his name and nationality were. When Chester told him his last name was Tanaka, the board interview said, "Oh, you're Japanese." Chester replied, "No, my parents are Japanese. I'm an American." The interviewer corrected him with the reply, "You're Japanese."

"Boy, my brother became agitated," Joe recalled. "The story goes that he reached across and was to grab this board member and says, 'Tell him I'm American.' But his friends restrained him fortunately."

The Army was no less racist in its approach to accepting the Tanaka brothers for service to their country. Joe and his brothers were placed among the other Nisei, second-generation Japanese Americans, in the now legendary 442nd Regiment composed entirely of men of Japanese descent.

Joe was sent to Arkansas, then Texas. His design background proved valuable to the Army, and he was assigned to creating models of terrain and other features that the Army could use for training purposes. He created charts to teach recruits about the operation of grenades and rifles before finally being sent overseas to Europe.

Waiting for him were his two brothers, who had enlisted in the Army in the meantime. Chester served with Company K of the 442nd, and Edward was a technical sergeant. Both participated in the intense battles to drive the Germans from Italy. Later, both Chester and Edward were sent to occupied Germany, where Edward was eventually charged with guarding German prisoners of war. Chester made headlines for being the first Japanese American soldier to be wounded in action. He received shrapnel wounds while fighting in Italy.

Chester would not be the only member of the 442nd to receive a Purple Heart for his service. The regiment suffered through some of the toughest fighting of the war and earned the name the Purple Heart Battalion primarily because of their actions in Italy. In December 1944, the War Department noted that of the 1,300 members of the Nisei Battalion, 1,000 of the men had received Purple Hearts for the wounds they received while fighting in the Italian campaigns. This was more Purple Hearts than any other battalion during the war. Its most famous action became known as the Rescue of the Lost Texas Battalion.

In October 1944, a battalion of 275 Texas National Guard soldiers became trapped behind enemy lines. They occupied a mountaintop but were surrounded on all sides by German artillery that was determined to eliminate the Texans. After learning of the Texans' predicament, American commanders paused their drive toward the Rhine River and redirected units toward the French mountain where the Texans were held up. Unfortunately, attempts to drive out the German units by means of heavy shelling did little since the heavy forests surrounding the mountain provided the Germans protection to withstand the American firepower. Two American infantry divisions also attempted to break through the German lines but could not endure the hail of German bullets raining down on them. Finally, the decision was made to call in the men of the 442nd Nisei Battalion.

During five days of intense, brutal fighting, the men of the 442nd succeeded in breaking through and opening the way for the Lost Texas Battalion to escape the mountain. The Nisei suffered hundreds of casualties but saved 211 of the 275 Texans. The action was lauded as the most heroic action of the 442nd and is generally recognized as one of the most important actions in US Army history. Among the soldiers fighting on the mountain was Chester Tanaka.

Letters written by Joe and Edward are held by The State Historical Society of Missouri. The surviving letters, including the one printed here, are written to good friends back in St. Louis. Joe's letter is lighthearted and funny as it tells of his time at Fort Benning, Georgia. Like many of his fellow soldiers, he was still adjusting to the demands of Army life and counting the days until it would be over.

Oct. 4, '44

Wed. nite

Hello Herb and Marion. Yes it is still Tanaka and he is still in O.C.S. This afternoon we had a G.T. in map reading.

GT= graded test. My first did all right. Tonight is our first free evening. Map reading is finished. Next subject riflemanship. Only 16 weeks and 18 GTs to go.

I've really been busy. Not enough hours in the day. Up at 6, in bed 11:30.

Yes, still concerned about my physical fitness. Herb, can you do 50 sit-ups? Can you do 30 push-ups? And brother you should see that obstacle wall.

However, day by day I am getting into condition. Soon I'll be able to get up from the table without collapsing. If I ever receive my bars, I will have to be carried from the platform because of exhaustion and surprise.

Well, Ed, is going into the Army in a few days. That makes 3 . . . the Tanaka boys are taking over.

I really didn't know what a setup I had in my previous camps whenever I carry my rifle I think of the pen I used to tote around the drawing board. When I think of an 18 hour day, 6 day wk (I wash clothes and equipment on Sun. morning) I think of 3-day passes. Well, only 18 GTs to go and 16 weeks to endure.

How's the hay fever, Herb? I've picked up a sniffle. Its from being thoroughly soaked from perspiration and letting it dry.

This is being written in the day room. The barracks lights go out at 10. The men then move into the latrine. You can't tell who is writing a letter or who is responding to a natural call.

I'll keep you posted.

Joe

After the war, Joe returned home to St. Louis. He became an instructor at the Washington University School of Architecture. Over the years, Joe supported the region's Japanese American community by becoming active in the Japanese American Citizens

League and advocating for the Asian community. On October 30, 1949, he and other veterans of the 442nd laid a wreath on the steps of the Soldiers Memorial downtown in observance of Nisei Soldiers Memorial Day, a day of remembrance of the rescue of the Lost Texas Battalion.

In 1981, Chester happened to see an exhibit at the Presidio Army Museum in San Francisco that featured the men of the 442nd. He had served as the battalion's historian since the war, recording the unit's history even as he fought his way across Europe. After seeing the Presidio's exhibit, Chester became actively involved in working to further commemorate his comrades through a larger history exhibit in collaboration with the Smithsonian Institution. He also kept the history of his battalion alive by writing *Go for Broke*, a pictorial history of the 442nd.

The story of the Tanaka brothers is a story of patriotism and perseverance. These three brothers rose up to serve their country and fight to uphold democratic ideals despite the hypocrisy that denied the civil rights of their fellow Japanese American citizens. They demonstrated their bravery in battle and won the respect of the nation. At the war's end, President Harry S. Truman honored the men of the 442nd in a special ceremony in Washington, DC. He awarded the unit the seventh Presidential Citation and told the soldiers present that day, "You fought not only the enemy, but you fought prejudice, and you won. Keep up the fight and you will make democracy stand for what it really means: the welfare of all the people, all the time."

Joe and Edward Tanaka are buried in Jefferson Barracks National Cemetery. Chester is buried in Hawaii.

On June 11, 1945, General Omar Bradley visited St. Louis and was received with a parade attended by 250,000 St. Louisans. *Collections of the Missouri Historical Society*

MISSOURI'S NUMBER ONE WAR HERO

On June 6, 1944, Missourian General Omar Bradley of the Twelfth Army commanded the troops storming Omaha Beach in the Normandy D-Day Invasion. Bradley was already a home state hero well before he made history during Operation Overlord. A year prior, his hometown of Moberly, Missouri, had proudly named its airport in his honor in a dedication ceremony attended by his wife, Mary, and their daughter, Elizabeth. Mary was also a Moberly native, and the town celebrated like a homecoming.

After the German surrender in 1945, Bradley, who one Moberly resident declared at the time as "Missouri's number one war hero," made a trip home to Missouri and was met with a rousing welcome. After first visiting his hometown of Moberly, Bradley arrived in St. Louis on June 11, 1945; the *Globe-Democrat* headline proclaimed, "250,000 Throng Acclaims Bradley Here." A parade led General Bradley to the steps of Soldiers Memorial, where he addressed the crowd. "I am sure this symbolized the way you feel about the men who are still over there." Then pointing to the site of the Court of Honor of World War II still under construction, he added, "Let us hope the one now building will be in honor of as few dead as possible."

When asked who was responsible for the victory over Germany, he said, "John Q Doughboy" and further noted that it was the home front and the Red Cross who played vital roles in defeating the European Axis powers.

Bradley was feted at a banquet at the Hotel Jefferson attended by Mayor Kaufman and 1,000 St. Louisans who were excited to see the general in person. It was a fitting tribute to a man who was considered to be a down-to-earth individual rather than an imposing figure such as Eisenhower.

After the war, Bradley was selected by fellow Missourian Harry S. Truman to lead the Veterans Administration, where he accomplished a great deal toward improving veterans' benefits, including strengthening the GI Bill. In 1948, Truman appointed him as the first chief of the Joint Chiefs of Staff. During the Korean War, Bradley was promoted to commander of the Army. He was only the fifth person to receive the rank. He retired from the service in 1953 but remained on active duty as commander of the Army until his death in 1981. At 69 years of service, he holds the longest record of duty in the American Armed Forces. General Omar Bradley is buried in Arlington National Cemetery.

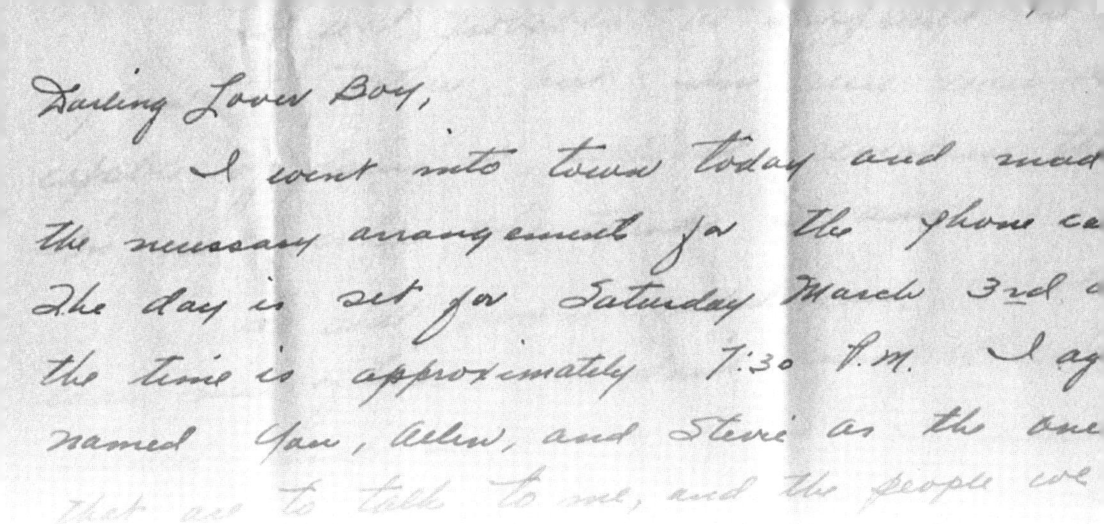

Darling Lover Boy,
I went into town today and mad
the necessary arrangements for the phone ca
The day is set for Saturday March 3rd a
the time is approximately 7:30 P.M. I a
named You, Allen, and Stevie as the one
that are to talk to me, and the people we

James Sherman letter, February 16, 1945. *Collections of the Missouri Historical Society*

"THE CENSORS WOULD NOT APPROVE ANY JEWISH CONVERSATION." — PETTY OFFICER JAMES SHERMAN, US NAVY

Censorship of servicemen's communications was not limited to letters and postcards. If a soldier or sailor was lucky enough to get access to a phone, they could arrange a phone call home, but this too had to be monitored. There were strict guidelines about what could or could not be said during a call. Like a letter, there could be no mention of where you were serving, nor could you discuss anything other than what topics you had preapproved when you arranged the call.

James Sherman made these arrangements to call home to St. Louis from his base in Hawaii, where he served as part of the Commander Destroyer Pacific at Pearl Harbor. One of the regulations stipulated before making a call was that everyone had to be identified for security purposes. It was an arduous process, and he had to send a letter home to his wife, Dottie, informing her of the protocol for the call. Completing all the details was difficult enough, but for James there was an added layer of complication for calling home. His mother, Etta, was not aware that he was serving outside the US. She had been kept in the dark about his whereabouts as a means of dispelling any fear on her behalf. However, James did want her to hear that he was safe. This brought up another problem. Etta spoke no English.

The Shermans were Ukrainian immigrants who had come to the United States when James was 11. As Ukrainian Jews, James's parents spoke Yiddish, as did everyone at home, but the Sherman children quickly learned to speak English through interactions outside their familial pod. For James, it was a necessity for his studies in the St. Louis Public Schools.

Being bilingual was not a problem in most situations, but not so when it came to military censorship. When James filled out the forms to arrange his phone call to his family, he listed his wife and young sons, Allen and Stevie, and he hoped to get his mother in on the conversation too, but he was told that this would not be possible. Yet, he still set to working out a plan to let her hear his voice while not breaking the rules. His instructions to Dottie (whom he referred to as Lover Boy in his letters) were clear, and she was tasked with making sure it all came together.

Friday, February 16, 1945

Darling Lover Boy,

I went into town today and made the necessary arrangements for the phone call. The day is set for Saturday March 3rd and the time is approximately 7:30 P.M. I again named you, Allen, and Stevie as the ones that are to talk to me, and the people aren't to mention are my mother, Lease, and Adolph. I wanted to name Mother as one who could talk to me, but the censor would not approve any Jewish conversation. It might be a good idea to have Mother at the house when I call, and squeeze her in to say "Hello James" or something like that, and I will answer her in English too. Also when she comes to the phone you need not say that she is coming to the phone. Just put her on the phone.

It will probably be difficult to explain to Mother, but I'm sure you are capable of doing so, without revealing that I'm not where she thinks I am.

I guess I have sort of adjusted my self to the Navy way of living, but honestly Darling, without you my life is empty. You are part of me, and I couldn't go on living without you for long. The thought of the future, when I come home to you, keeps me going.

I was glad to hear that you plan to take your vacation with your cousin and others. I didn't want you to go alone. Some one might steal you from me, and that would be just like losing my life. I love you that much.

Well sweet, time to say Good Night again, and you will always have

All my love,

Jimmy

How did the call go? We can only wonder. Besides the hoops one had to jump through to call home, there was also the cost of making a long-distance call. The three-minute call cost around $9 in 1944. This is approximately equivalent to $162 in 2025.

James was released from his naval service in February 1945.

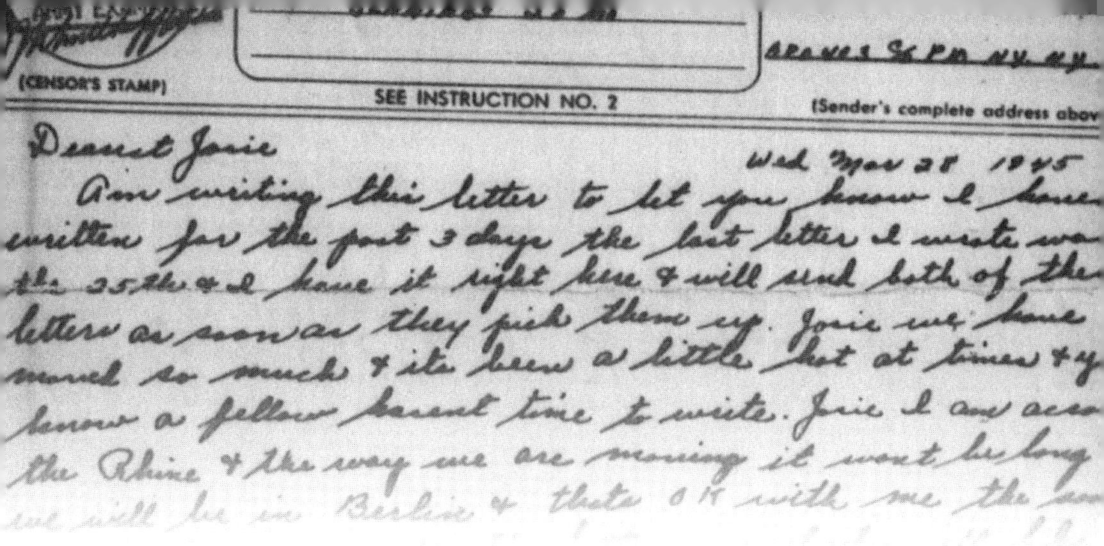

(CENSOR'S STAMP)

SEE INSTRUCTION NO. 2

(Sender's complete address abov

Dearest Josie

Wed Mar 28 1945

Am writing this letter to let you know I have
written for the past 3 days the last letter I wrote was
the 25th & I have it right here & will send both of the
letters as soon as they pick them up. Josie we have
moved so much & its been a little hot at times & y
know a fellow hasnt time to write. Josie I am acro
the Rhine & the way we are moving it wont be long
we will be in Berlin & thats OK with me the

PFC Peter Oleski V-mail, March 28, 1945. *Collections of the Missouri Historical Society*

"WE WILL BE IN BERLIN & THAT'S OK WITH ME." — PFC PETER OLESKI, US ARMY

Peter Oleski was a 27-year-old warehouse worker in the spring of 1943 when he was inducted into the Army. He had spent the last seven years sorting fruit for distribution to the local A&P grocery stores around the city. It wasn't long before Peter was far from the produce warehouse and thrust into the thick of combat in Europe. As a member of Battery A, 549th Anti-Aircraft Artillery Automatic Weapons Battalion, Peter's responsibility was to keep the lines of battle communications open by operating the switchboard in combat, under fire, between artillery guns.

By March 1945, the last stiff resistance by the German Army had crumbled after Hitler's gamble with the push at the Ardennes. Peter had survived the Battle of the Bulge, and now he and his battalion had crossed the Rhine River into the fatherland. They were taking the fight to Hitler, and there was a sense of excitement that this long, costly war in Europe was about to come to an end.

Peter's V-mail home to Josie, as he called his wife, on March 28, 1945, is filled with hope that, like Berlin, the end was in sight. You can sense the excitement in Peter's words and reassurances that he would come through and return home. He was looking to the future and "an addition to our family."

> To Mrs. Josephine Oleski
> 5742 Albia Terrance
> Jennings 20 MO
>
> Wed, March 28 1945
>
> Am writing this letter to let you know I haven't written for the past 3 days. The last letter I wrote was the 25th and I have it right here & will send both of these letters as soon as they pick them up. Josie we have moved so much & it has been a little hot at times & you know a fellow hasn't time to write. Josie I am across the Rhine & the way we are moving it won't be long & we will be in Berlin & thats ok with me. The sooner we get this over with the better everybody will like it. I am in good health & hope this letter finds you & the baby well. Honey this mo. is just about over & then one more mo. to go & I know you are as anxious for this to be over with & we will have an addition to our family . . .
>
> Now don't worry if you don't hear from me for a few days at a time as I write every chance I git & there are times I can't. I will close with loads of love to you both. God bless you both, your loving husband,
>
> Pete

When Peter returned home, the family did grow. Eventually Pete and Josephine had four children. Sadly, Peter did not live a long life. He passed away at the age of 48 in 1965. He is buried in Calvary Cemetery in St. Louis.

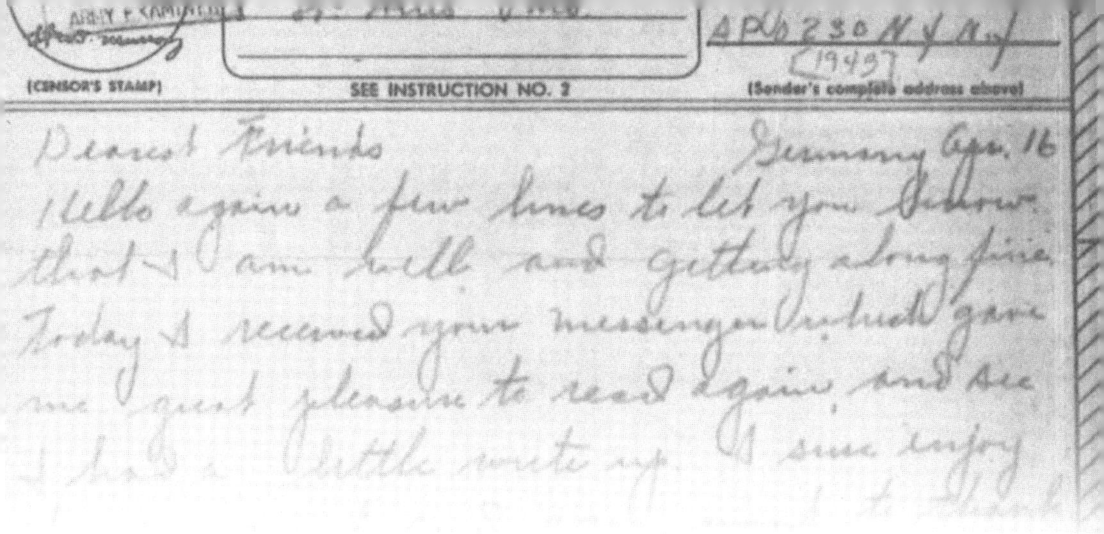

(CENSOR'S STAMP) SEE INSTRUCTION NO. 2 (Sender's complete address above)

Dearest Friends Germany Apr. 16

Hello again a few lines to let you know that I am well and getting along fine. Today I received your messenger which gave me great pleasure to read again, and see ... little write up. I sure enjoy

Joseph F. Criest V-mail, April 16, 1945. *The State Historical Society of Missouri*

"SURE WAS A BLOW TO US ALL WHEN WE LOST OUR GREAT LEADER."

— SERGEANT JOSEPH F. CRIEST, US ARMY

At 11 a.m. on April 14, 1945, the city of St. Louis paused and went silent for two minutes. Mayor Aloys Kaufmann stood in silence on the south steps of Soldiers Memorial before a crowd of 4,000 St. Louisans. A steady rain fell, and Kaufmann looked out over a forest of black umbrellas. It was a fitting scene that reflected the solemn mood as Kaufmann led the vigil to mourn the death of Franklin Delano Roosevelt. The previous day, the nation had been jarred by the news that the president had died at his winter home in Warm Springs, Georgia. The *Post-Dispatch* reported that the news had left people in stunned silence. For both supporters and detractors alike it had to sink in that this man, a leader who often seemed bigger than life and who had led the country for 12 years, was now gone.

Mayor Kaufmann ordered that a complete halt to all business be observed for two minutes on that Saturday at 11 a.m. Even the lines of Southwestern Bell telephone went silent. St. Louisans of all communities, ethnicities, and faiths joined together on that rainy morning. Clergymen from several of the city's houses of worship provided a prayer and words of faith to those present. Monsignor John P. Cody of the St. Louis Archdiocese delivered the invocation. The Reverend Joseph Frenz of the Bethlehem Lutheran Church read the president's favorite Bible verses from First Corinthians. Reverend W. J. G. McLin of the Colored Episcopal Methodist Church used his time to declare, "No man with his noble social ideas could ever die. I, with my people, will never accept that he is dead. He will become more alive as the ages roll away." Then the ceremony ended with a benediction given by Rabbi Julius Gordon of Shaare Emeth.

But this memorial was only one of many held in churches and halls across the region. The whole country was in mourning, as were the men and women fighting overseas. For most young soldiers, Roosevelt's leadership was all they ever knew. He had led them through the dark days of Pearl Harbor, and now when the end of the war in Europe seemed imminent, he was gone.

Sergeant Joseph Criest noted the loss in this letter home to Father Prokes at St. John Nepomuk. Criest, the only son of Czech and Bulgarian immigrants Bessie and Anthony Criest, was a truck driver before the war. His family were working-class St. Louisans: hardworking, God-fearing, and patriotic, but usually the first to feel the financial strains when the economy took a turn for the worse. Roosevelt's New Deal created programs like Social Security and unemployment benefits for families like the Criests, and he earned their reverence in return.

Criest returned home after the war to a country that was both stronger and more stable due to Roosevelt's programs. The GI Bill, signed by Roosevelt in 1944, would further add to that stability by providing free education, home loans, and other benefits to returning servicemen and women that fueled decades of economic progress.

> V-Mail
>
> To: The Home Front
> St. John Nep Church
> St. Louis, MO
> From: Sgt. Jos. F Criest
> Bty B 957 F.A.
> APO 230 NY NY
>
> Germany Apr 16
>
> Dear Friends
>
> Hello again a few lines to let you know that I am well and getting along fine. Today I received your messenger which gave me great pleasure to read again and see I had a little write up. I sure enjoy it very much and again want to thank you. At the present I am pretty busy. Driving on toward Berlin and victory and hope it is soon. Sure was a blow to us all when we lost our great leader. Sure wish I could run across some of the boys from back home but so far haven't had much luck. Have seen some beautiful country lately.
>
> Bye for now, God bless you all, will write again.
>
> As Always, Joe

Sergeant Criest's letter declares, "Driving on toward Berlin and victory." His confidence was not misplaced by the time this was written on April 16. As he penned these words, Soviet troops were entering Berlin. Savage street-to-street fighting broke out, carried out not only by Hitler's remaining SS troops but also by hastily conscripted teenage boys and old men in a last-ditch effort to protect the German capital.

As a field artilleryman, Criest endured combat in France, Belgium, and Germany. He was presented with a Bronze Star in June 1945 for meritorious service in direct support of combat operations against the enemy. Just briefly after his return from the war, he married his sweetheart, Ruth Fulgham. Joseph Criest died in 1979. He is buried next to Ruth in Resurrection Cemetery in Affton.

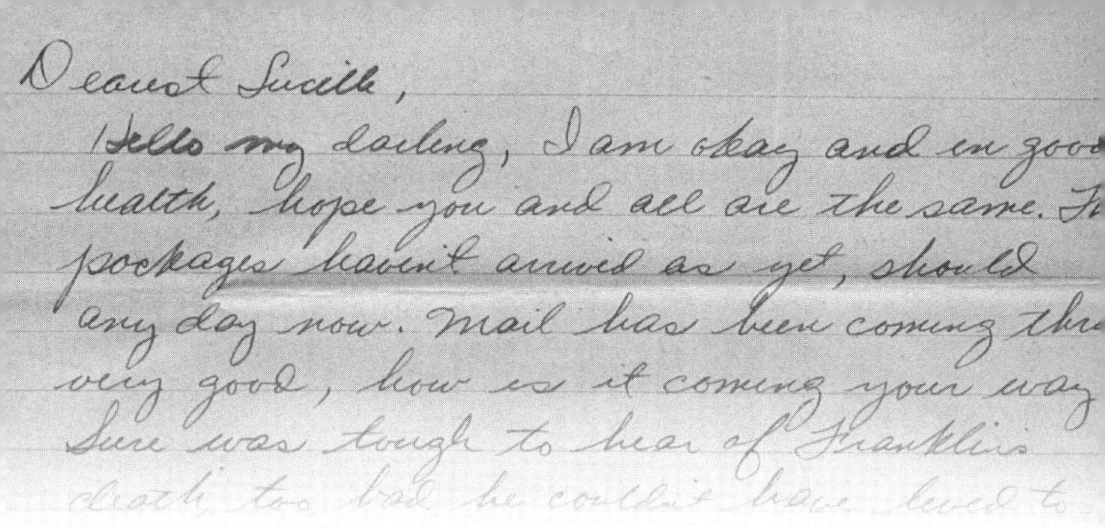

Dearest Lucille,
Hello my darling, I am okay and in goo
health, hope you and all are the same. T
packages haven't arrived as yet, should
any day now. Mail has been coming thr
very good, how is it coming your wa
Sure was tough to hear of Franklin's
death, too bad he couldn't have lived to

Francis Weidler letter, April 15, 1945. *Collections of the Missouri Historical Society*

"TO [SIC] BAD HE COULDN'T HAVE LIVED TO SEE IT." — FRANCIS WEIDLER, US ARMY

Like Joseph Criest, Francis Charles Weidler was saddened by the news of Franklin Roosevelt's passing. Weidler, a censor in the Army Air Force stationed in France, wrote home to his fiancée, Lucille Simons, commenting on the president's death and the effect the news had in France. French leader Charles de Gaulle, despite often being at odds with Roosevelt, was still greatly affected by the president's death and declared a week of mourning in France. He would later write to President Truman and declare of Roosevelt that "all of France loved him."

In Great Britain, Prime Minister Winston Churchill provided a deeply personal eulogy before the Houses of Parliament five days after Roosevelt's death. Churchill, who more than any other leader was a close personal friend of the president, said of Roosevelt, "His love of his own country, his respect for its constitution, his power of gauging the tides and currents of its mobile public opinion, were always evident, but, added to these, were the beatings of that generous heart which was always stirred to anger and to action by spectacles of aggression and oppression by the strong against the weak. It is, indeed, a loss, a bitter loss to humanity that those heart-beats are stilled forever."

Weidler's observations of the aftermath of Roosevelt's passing are very telling of the atmosphere of the time and reflect the deep connection that many felt to one of America's most influential and charismatic modern leaders.

April 15

France

Dearest Lucille,

Hello my darling, I am okay and in good health, hope you and all are the same. The packages haven't arrived as yet, should any day now. Mail has been coming thru very good, how is it coming your way? Sure was tough to hear of Franklin's death, too bad he couldn't have lived to see it thru, everything in France here paid homage to him today, the boys who went on pass say most all the cafes were closed, and they usually have dances at some of these little towns on Saturday and Sundays, they were stopped too.

We stood in ranks this afternoon to pay our respects, five minutes of silence after we heard a message from the Secretary of War, read by one of our officers. I read in the Stars and Stripes where they held big church sermons for him, Catholic, Protestant & Jewish, it was by far the worse news we have heard in a long time. With Harry Truman in his place won't have much to do with the war situation, that was all planned before Roosevelt's death that is my belief anyway.

Well my dear I must close for now, more later. Hope you get loads of mail.

I love you,
Buddy

News of Roosevelt's passing, in Weidler's opinion, was "the worse news we have heard in a long time," but this echoed the feelings of many US soldiers and sailors. How this might affect the war was certainly on their minds, but Stewart was certainly right in his assumption that the war would not be affected very much since most of the planning had been finalized during Roosevelt's presidency. Truman inherited Roosevelt's strategy and followed it. However, he had little choice since Roosevelt had kept Truman in the dark on much of the war's planning, including informing him of the work on the atomic bomb.

Truman's legacy would largely be shaped by his influence on postwar planning. Roosevelt's war strategies and the generals he put in place had done their job. The war in Europe ended less than a month later after his death. As Weidler expressed, "Too bad he couldn't have lived to see it thru."

Francis Charles Weidler returned to St. Louis and married Lucille. He worked for American Stove Company and died in 1987. He is buried in Resurrection Cemetery in Affton.

'Daddy's in Germany'

escribes Horrors of Buchenwald Camp
In Letter to Wife

As soon as Master Sgt. Eben T. Bradbury reads this
blication, after it has reached him somewhere in Germany,
will know that yesterday the writer talked with his 2½-
ar-old son who scarcely remembers his dad but who never-
eless talks about him practically all the time. He will know
at his son is quite aware of where his dad is because he
id, when asked by his grandmother, "He's in Germany
d he's got a Bronze Star."

What young Stuart Trask Brad-
ry didn't realize were the horrors
the infamous Buchenwald con-
ntration camp which his dad, a
rmer Emerson employe, helped to

Voice of Emerson, May 1945. *Collections of Missouri Historical Society*

"WHATEVER THEY HAVE SAID ABOUT THE PLACE COULDN'T POSSIBLY BE ENOUGH."

— MASTER SERGEANT EBEN T. BRADBURY, US ARMY

Eben Trask Bradbury Jr. grew up on Westminster Place in St. Louis. His father held a senior position at a box factory, and the family enjoyed a pleasant middle-class life. Eben attended Soldan High School and then Washington University before spending time at the University of Freiberg in Germany. In November 1941, less than a month before Pearl Harbor, in a morning ceremony in the

Crystal Room of the Coronado Hotel, Eben married Rosemary Cave. They moved into their home on Eager Road. Soon they had a son, Stuart.

Eben entered the Army in 1943. He was sent to the European Theater and assigned to military intelligence, likely due to his time spent in Germany, and he traveled as a photographer and interpreter with the First Army.

On April 11, 1945, the men of the Third Army's 6th Armored Division rolled up to the gates of Buchenwald concentration camp. It became the first camp to be liberated. The horrors that met the men of the Super Sixth, as the division was known, haunted them. The survivors flocked to them as the soldiers attempted to grasp what they were seeing. The piles of bodies, the stench of death, and the presence of the gas chambers and incinerators were almost too much for the Americans to comprehend. The next day General Eisenhower arrived to inspect the camp and see for himself the conditions described to him. When he finished, he stated, "We are told that the American soldier does not know what he is fighting for. Now, at least, we know what he is fighting against."

It became clear to Master Sergeant Bradbury who he was fighting against when the soldiers broke through and opened the gates. He saw unimaginable horrors.

The following is reprinted from *The Voice of Emerson*, the

Master Sgt. Eben T. Bradbury served as a photographer and interpreter for the First Army. He received the Bronze Star for his service. *Collections of the Missouri Historical Society*

newsletter of Emerson Electric.

I suppose you have read about it. Whatever they have said about the place couldn't possibly have been enough nor can anything I say. You would have to see it to appreciate it. According to some of the guys we talked to, this is one of the better camps, too. That is the amazing part of it.

All the time the people were there they were efficiently organized. There were no nationalistic tendencies and no disputes. Among French, Russian, Czech, Yugoslav, Italian, Belgian, Dutch, German and prisoners of 18 other countries there were complete unison against the Nazis. Not open revolt but completely passive unobtrusive resistance.

Small arms and ammunition were smuggled into the camp and kept hidden for 'the day.' Finally it arrived and the leaders were hard pressed to keep the thousands quiet. They heard the American artillery come closer and closer, yet raised not a finger in revolt. The Nazis made plans to evacuate the whole lot, an absolute impossible task through their physical fitness.

Finally machine gun and rifle fire came over the hills and they struck. They captured 140 of the SS guards without any trouble. By the time the Yanks arrived they were in complete control of the camp and had their own organization set up, headed by a German political prisoner.

A great many have died since the Yanks arrived. There are a great many others who are beyond help and will very soon die. Today I saw three large incinerators still filled with the charred bones and human bodies. I saw the scaffold where they hung them in threes by the thousands before burning them. These are no rumors or propaganda tales.

You perhaps wonder just what crime a man had to commit to get in the place.

I'll tell you about one of these young Yugoslavs, who is probably a pretty typical case. One evening, four years ago, he was walking in Belgrade. Somewhere in the neighborhood a German soldier was shot. The area, not the house, not the block, but the area in which the crime was committed was surrounded and all males picked up. The first 100 were shot on the spot. The rest were transported to Germany to work and die for the Supermen. That is why, somewhere in Yugoslavia, the mother whose boy, then 17, didn't come home to supper that night, doesn't know to this day what happened to him. His was a great crime.

Account by Master Sgt. Eben T. Bradbury, photographic interpreter, First Army.

Bradbury's descriptions would mirror those experienced by other Allied soldiers who liberated camps in Germany and Poland. Another St. Louisan, Ralph Barrale, served with the 821st Military Police Unit, one of the companies that liberated Dachau. He noted in an interview he provided in 2018 at the age of 94 that many of his fellow soldiers, even throughout the time they spent fighting against the Germans, questioned why they were fighting in Europe when it was the Japanese who had attacked the United States, not the Germans. Those opinions changed when they discovered the atrocities at Dachau. "Well, we found out why we were over there," said Barrale. When he and his men saw the atrocities committed there, "then we knew why we were there, and the whole world knew why we were there." They were there to destroy the Germans and not let this happen again anywhere else.

Master Sergeant Eben T. Bradbury received the Bronze Star for his service in Britain, France, and Germany. He returned home after the war but died young. Bradbury passed away in 1958 at the age of 43. He is buried in Bellefontaine Cemetery.

Patsy Dunn holds up the *St. Louis Star-Times* in two photos, one at the war's beginning and one at its end. The duration of the war is captured by how much she had grown during the war years. *Collections of the Missouri Historical Society*

THE END IS NEAR

It was clear that the Germans were near defeat in the spring of 1945. News of the Soviet advance through Berlin and Hitler's subsequent suicide spelled the end of the Third Reich. Roosevelt's plan to focus all attention on defeating the European Axis powers had paid off, but he hadn't lived to see it. At 2:41 a.m. on May 7, German Admiral Karl Doenitz, who was the acting leader of the German Reich upon the death of Hitler, ordered Wehrmacht General Gustaf Alfred Jodl to go to the Allied Supreme Command Headquarters in Reims, France, to sign the documents imposing the unconditional surrender of Germany.

The Supreme Headquarters was not some grand edifice but rather a nondescript red-brick school building. General Dwight Eisenhower was not present to meet Jodl or see the signing.

Eisenhower's chief of staff presented the papers along with Soviet and English generals. With a stroke of the pen, five years and eight months of some of the most intense and brutal warfare in modern history was over.

Some persistent Nazi generals sought to continue fighting in several isolated pockets of Europe, but most Germans were done with the war. Berlin lay in ruins, the country's infrastructure was destroyed, and hunger was rampant. The atrocities of the Holocaust were becoming known to all, and the occupation of the country by Allied forces brought all manner of challenges. There was much work to be done.

Back home, President Harry S. Truman declared the observance of V-E Day to begin at 8 a.m. on May 8. When the time arrived, the president broadcast a message from Washington followed by Mayor Kaufmann's message to St. Louis. When they finished, air raid sirens blared, and church bells rang. Schools, stores, taverns, and government offices were closed. The *Globe* reported that workers at downtown office buildings rained down paper and confetti from the windows above, but, noted by a reporter, the amount of celebration did not equal that of the news of when the Armistice for World War I was announced in the city.

The one segment of the city that did not shut down was the war materials plants. The workers continued their daily routine producing planes, tanks, and ammunition because while Germany was defeated, Japan fought on. During his radio address, President Truman used his time to comment on Japan's fate. He urged them to face the inevitable and surrender rather than continue to fight and die.

After the sun went down, the bright lights of St. Louis came on again after years of nighttime blackouts. It was a moment of joy for many, but hundreds of St. Louis families were left knowing that their sons would not return. Amidst the news of victory, the *Globe* ran a sobering headline: "War in Europe cost US Army 732,270 Casualties." It was a tremendous price and a bitter reminder that an unbridled obedience to dictators and despots leads nowhere but to destruction and death.

As thrilling as the end of the war with Germany was, there was still another job to do. On the marquee of radio station KWK next door to the Fox Theatre, the station's sign blazed, "On to Tokyo." The V-E celebrations were tempered a bit by knowing that there was still a lot of fighting yet to do and that more men would lose their lives in the Pacific before anyone could really celebrate.

Everyone turned their full attention to the war in the Pacific. It was common knowledge that the Japanese were fighting a losing battle, but they were still fighting, and few saw an easy end to the war. Yet, known to only a handful of people in St. Louis (those with the right national security credentials), materials were processed at Mallinckrodt Chemical Company on the city's north side that just might hold the key to the end of the war. Uranium was processed to become the fuel for a new weapon—a single bomb that would unleash power and destruction on a scale never seen before in the history of mankind.

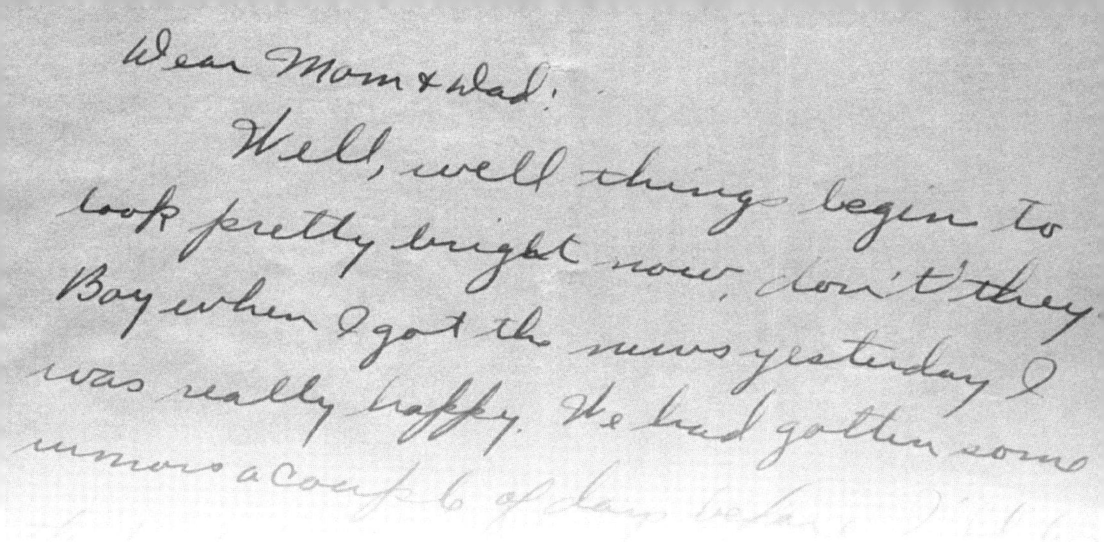
Dear Mom & Dad!
Well, well things begin to look pretty bright now, don't they.
Boy when I got the news yesterday I was really happy. We had gotten some rumors a couple of days before

Seaman John Vernon Pratt letter, August 16, 1945. *Collections of the Missouri Historical Society*

"WELL, WELL THINGS BEGIN TO LOOK PRETTY BRIGHT NOW, DON'T THEY?"

— SEAMAN 1ST CLASS JOHN VERNON PRATT, US NAVY

---

16 Aug 1945
Day after Nips surrender
A wonderful day

Dear Mom & Dad!

Well, well things begin to look pretty bright now, don't they? Boy when I got the news yesterday I was really happy. We had gotten some rumors a couple of days before. I'll bet the people back there really celebrated. We couldn't celebrate, we just had to take it quietly. It sure surprised me to hear that they were quiet so soon. I always said it would probably be 18 months after Germany. But I sure am glad it's over. Now I can start worrying about how long it's going to take before I get home. I haven't the slightest idea how long it will be.

Lots of love,

Always,

Vern

Seaman Vern Pratt summed up the feelings of all American servicemen with this simple phrase added to the date line of this letter home to his parents: "A wonderful day." The war was over. Japan had surrendered, and Pearl Harbor had been avenged. America had won a two-front war. It was an amazing thing to consider.

It wasn't enough that President Truman had inherited the presidency during one of the most challenging events in the nation's history, but unbeknownst to him, he also had inherited the world's most destructive weapon. Roosevelt had not shared any knowledge of the Manhattan Project with Truman, so it was a total surprise to learn of this weapon that could level nearly an entire city. When they informed him of the plan, no one even knew if the bomb would really work. Whether the atomic chain reaction they had predicted would commence was entirely theoretical, but in July 1945, a horrific mushroom cloud grew up out of the New Mexico desert. The atomic bomb was born, and now Truman faced the question of whether to drop it on a Japanese city.

For the entirety of the war, it had been assumed that if the Allies achieved superiority over the Japanese, the final push to defeat them would rest on an invasion of mainland Japan. The Imperial Japanese, it was believed, would do everything in their power to protect the Japanese Emperor Hirohito, whom they saw as divine, and to avoid suffering the indignity of having an occupying force on

A B-29 Superfortress drops its bombs on an unidentified Japanese port city. Two B-29s, the *Enola Gay* and *Bockscar*, would drop the atomic bombs on Hiroshima and Nagasaki in August 1945. *Collections of the Missouri Historical Society*

Japanese soil. Military commanders estimated that such a landing would cost the lives of perhaps hundreds of thousands of Allied soldiers. They envisioned street-to-street combat through cities and guerrilla warfare in the Japanese countryside. Still, military planners were contemplating plans for an invasion, and American airpower was preparing for just such a thing by pounding Japan's industrial cities with daily firebombing. Japanese civilian death totals were rising day by day, and the Imperial navy's sea and air defenses were all but exhausted. Yet no one predicted that the end would come quickly or easily.

Truman made the fateful decision to drop the bomb. He saw it as a way of ending the war more quickly and saving the lives of countless American soldiers and sailors. On August 6, 1945, an American Air Force B-29 Superfortress bomber, the *Enola Gay*, flew over Hiroshima at 8:15 a.m. and released an atomic bomb named "Little Boy" that held the equivalent of 15,000 tons of TNT. It detonated 1,800 feet above the city. With a blinding flash, five square miles of the city were instantly leveled, and a firestorm burned what was left. It killed 80,000 people nearly instantly, while others suffered from terrible burns and radiation poisoning and died in the following days. The final total death count was 140,000.

The Japanese were given an ultimatum to surrender unconditionally. Three days passed, and they did not respond, so on August 9, another B-29 took off from an airstrip on the island of Tinian in the Pacific. Its destination was Kokura, a main industrial city, but when the American pilot reached Kokura, he found the city was hidden under heavily overcast skies, so he chose the next city of Nagasaki.

On board the B-29, named *Bockscar*, was a larger atomic bomb called "Big Boy" weighing 10,000 pounds and packing the power of 22,000 tons of TNT. The pilot released the second bomb at two minutes after 11:00 a.m., and another 60,000 people died in Nagasaki.

Emperor Hirohito declared the surrender of Japan on August 15, 1945. On September 2, 1945, aboard the USS *Missouri*, representatives of Imperial Japan signed the formal terms of surrender under the watch of US General Douglas MacArthur.

With the war's end, America's fighting men were ready to come home. It would take months for the Army and Navy to release those who qualified for discharge. For sailors like Vern Pratt, the end could not come soon enough. Though he was not released until early in 1946, when it was over he returned to St. Louis and found lifetime employment with the Missouri Pacific Railroad.

John Vernon Pratt passed away in 2008. He is buried in Jefferson Barracks National Cemetery.

An impromptu parade through downtown immediately after President Truman announced the Japanese surrender on the evening of August 15, 1945. *Collections of the Missouri Historical Society*

V-J DAY IN ST. LOUIS

On August 14, rumors were circulating around the city that the end was near. Some office workers downtown were celebrating early by dumping showers of paper from the high-rise buildings while flag vendors began to set up on street corners, but by the end of the afternoon, there was still no good news. Then came a message from the White House that President Truman would make a special announcement at 6 p.m. Everyone anxiously waited for words from Truman and gathered around the closest radio.

Truman then read the statement everyone had waited nearly five years to hear: "I have received this afternoon a message from the Japanese government . . . I deem this reply a full acceptance of the Potsdam declaration which specifies the unconditional surrender of Japan."

Almost immediately the streets of downtown were filled

with crowds of jubilant St. Louisans, and cars ran bumper to bumper through the streets, horns honking. "Central figures in every group," noted the *Post-Dispatch*, "were the men in uniform, returned veterans, and recent recruits alike." They were rushed by well-wishers and some "led the jubilation and collected kisses from every pretty girl within reach, and others not so alluring."

In Soulard, the celebrations were in full swing around St. John Nepomuk too. Father Prokes reported in the *Messenger* that upon hearing the announcement, "In a minute or two the horns started to blare on 12th St and then bedlam broke loose." The people of the neighborhood jumped in their cars, and those who couldn't ride inside stood on the running boards and waved "anything from flags to toilet paper and rags." City buses were jammed with riders ringing cowbells and cheering.

While most cheered with happiness, others saw it as bittersweet. "It's fun for them," Prokes heard one woman say, "but my boy won't be coming back from the Pacific."

That night, many crowded St. John's to attend Mass and thank God for peace, noted Father Prokes. It was the same across the city. Temple Israel and Christ Church Cathedral held services. Second Baptist Church at Kingshighway and Washington had a crowd of 100 arrive to celebrate and pray, and at St. John's Methodist Church, an Army captain was married by candlelight.

Downtown a dance was spontaneously arranged in Memorial Plaza. The Jefferson Barracks band played for the crowd, and local radio personalities and performers showed up to sing and celebrate. It was a perfect night, reported the *Post-Dispatch*: "The night was warm, a gentle breeze blew from the south and a half-moon, veiled by wisps of clouds, lighted the festivities."

In the same edition of the *Post-Dispatch* ran a headline: "Armed services to send 7 million back to civilian life in a year." With the return of so many, times would change. The city would change, and life would change for everyone forever.

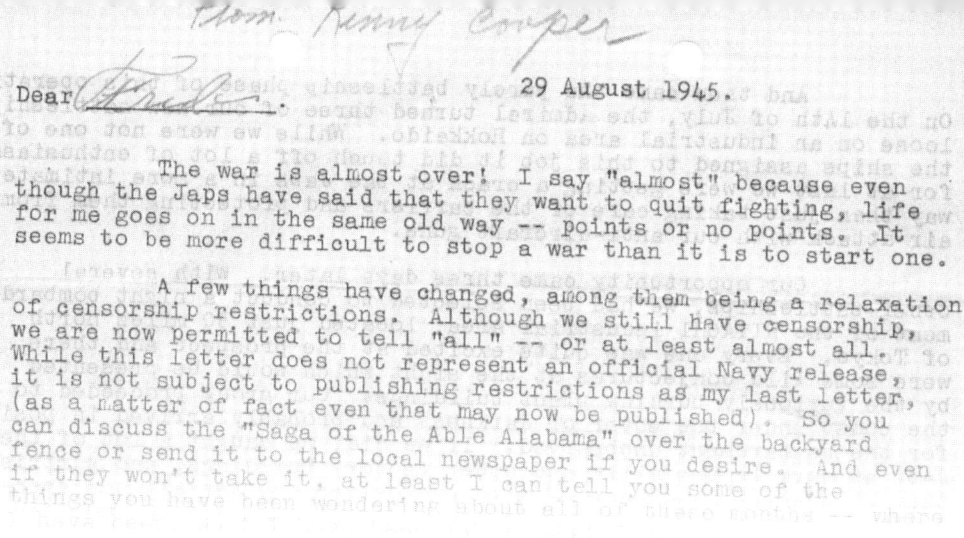
From: Kenny Cooper

Dear Fred:

29 August 1945.

The war is almost over! I say "almost" because even though the Japs have said that they want to quit fighting, life for me goes on in the same old way -- points or no points. It seems to be more difficult to stop a war than it is to start one.

A few things have changed, among them being a relaxation of censorship restrictions. Although we still have censorship, we are now permitted to tell "all" -- or at least almost all. While this letter does not represent an official Navy release, it is not subject to publishing restrictions as my last letter, (as a matter of fact even that may now be published). So you can discuss the "Saga of the Able Alabama" over the backyard fence or send it to the local newspaper if you desire. And even if they won't take it, at least I can tell you some of the things you have been wondering about all of these months -- where

Kenneth Cooper letter, February 29, 1943. *St. Charles Historical Society*

"I AM ABOARD THE USS *ALABAMA*, THE 'PRIDE OF THE NAVY.'"

— SEAMAN 1ST CLASS KENNETH ALEXANDER COOPER, US NAVY

The USS *Alabama* (BB-60) rests today in Mobile Bay, Alabama, one of the few surviving mighty battleships from World War II. In American naval history, it is a legendary ship that saw service in both the Atlantic and the Pacific, first battling the German fleet in the frigid waters of the North Atlantic and then steaming into the Pacific and witnessing some of the fiercest battles waged against the Imperial Japanese.

One of the "Mighty A" sailors was a young former truck

driver from St. Charles, Missouri, named Kenneth Cooper. Ken or Kenny was proud of his service in the Navy, and to his credit he chronicled his time for posterity. In August 1945, after the Japanese surrender allowed most of the censorship restrictions to be lifted, he wrote the following form letter, which he sent to his friends and family. "We are now permitted to tell 'all' or at least almost all," Kenny wrote to Frederick Tainter, publisher of the St. Charles *Bugle*, a newspaper started by Tainter and sent to St. Charles County servicemen serving at home and abroad. Kenny had written Tainter in 1943 to thank him for sending him the *Bugle*, saying, "It gives me a lot of pleasure & also keeps a fellow informed where his friends are & how things are progressing." He added, "You are undoubtedly wondering where I am," but noted "that, of course, is a military secret."

But now the veil was lifted, and Kenny provided Tainter with a very accurate and complete history of the *Alabama*'s service during his time onboard. The *Alabama*, Kenny noted at the time of writing, was waiting along with the rest of Admiral Halsey's Third Fleet off the coast of Japan "waiting for the peace arrangements to be made." He promised Fred that once he was able and after the peace ceremony had concluded, he would write another account of what he had witnessed.

General Douglas MacArthur led the formal signing of the Japanese surrender aboard the USS *Missouri*, September 2, 1945, formally ending World War II. *National Archives*

The letter here is excerpted due to its length, but Kenny does an excellent job of chronicling the story of the "Mighty A." He begins:

> August 29, 1945
>
> Dear Fred.
>
> The war is almost over. I say "almost" because even though the Japs have said that they want to quit fighting, life for me goes on in the same old way—points or no points. It seems to be more difficult to stop a war than it is to start one.

He then proceeded to tell the story of the *Alabama*'s service starting after the Battle of Leyte Gulf.

> We got underway from Leyte Gulf on Sunday, July 1, shortly after we departed, all of us were informed that we were going north to conduct sustained attacks on the Japanese empire home islands. From the plans it was quite apparent that Admiral Halsey was really determined to knock the blazes out of the Japs, 4 included in his intentions were orders for the battleships to steam right up to the Japanese coast and bombard some of the choice industrial targets which were extremely valuable to the Japs. This was something new for it had never been done before. Frankly it made most of us a little bit more serious for all we have had an acquaintance with the Jap kamikazes. We really started training in earnest.

Kenny's account begins with the *Alabama*'s departure from Leyte Gulf in the Philippines. There the ship had played a major role in the Battle of Leyte Gulf, the last major naval battle of the war, and the Allied victory that allowed the Americans to finally land in the Philippines. After defeating the Japanese navy, the *Alabama* and the Third Fleet patrolled the Philippine waters and endured a violent typhoon. Kenny doesn't mention this, but it had to have been

The USS *Alabama* was launched in 1942. Kenny Cooper would note that during its time at sea during the war it would "steam 207,000 sea miles." *National Archives*

seared in his memory. Known facetiously as Halsey's Typhoon, the admiral had underestimated the strength of the storm and chose to ride it out. The winds and waves soon became overwhelming, and the Americans lost three destroyers and more than 800 men to the typhoon. Other ships were damaged and scattered.

The kamikazes were some of the biggest worries for the sailors as described in Kenny's account. At Leyte, the Japanese began to use the suicide pilots in organized attacks. Swarms of kamikaze planes attacked Allied ships during the battle. It was a testament to just how depleted and desperate the Japanese had become in the final months of the war. Kamikaze attacks had become one of the last defenses for the Japanese as they were unable to produce the bombs, planes, and ammunition needed to repel the American advance. They also had lost most of their experienced pilots who could engage in effective air-to-air combat with American flyers. Therefore, they resorted to using poorly trained suicide pilots in a hammer-like strategy rather than utilizing skilled surgical attacks.

The lack of any substantive counterattack by the Japanese in the summer of 1945 even surprised Kenny and his fellow crewmen, who expected nothing less than an all-out assault on the *Alabama* as the Navy got ever closer to the Japanese home islands.

> By the 10th of July, the task force was in position and ready to go to work. Planes from the carriers started raking Jap the islands from Nagasaki to Hakodate, and by the time we got up as far north as Hokkaido the Japs had been severely mauled, and all of us were completely amazed. You see none of our expectations had worked out. Only a few Jap planes had come near the force and things were really easy. Of course, the carrier planes had been finding lots of Jap planes, but they were mostly on the ground and as you have probably noted in the various communiques, those carrier planes really destroyed thousands of Jap aircraft. The whole thing seemed to be repetition of our Filipina tax last fall. Each time we set out on a strike, we always said, "This is it. This time they will really come out." But they never did. Nor did they this time.

The American bombing of Japanese ports and bases on the mainland seriously crippled their ability to strike back.

> As a matter of fact the pilots practically ran out of targets, because they were out principally to get airfields and planes. The remnants of the Jap Fleet were no worry to us, but when there didn't seem to be any more air facilities to attack, the planes were put to work on what was left of the Jap Fleet and the results were great for they completed the destruction of the Navy. They even sank the railroad ferries which connect the island of Hokkaido with Honshu, a very serious loss to Jap industry.

While the military and scientists back in the US secretly made the final tests on the atomic bomb, the Navy was still preparing for the planned invasion of Japan. Battleships such as the *Alabama* were to play an essential role in this strategy by softening Japanese mainland defenses and production. Kenny explained:

> . . . and then came the purely battleship phase of this operation. On the 14th of July, the Admiral turned three

of our new battleships loose on an industrial area on Hokkaido. While we were not one of the ships assigned to do this job it did touch off a lot of enthusiasm for at last we were getting a crack at the Jap in a more intimate way than just taking care of the carriers and protecting them from air attack with our anti-aircraft guns.

Our opportunity came three days later. With several other battleships we had been selected to conduct a night bombardment of the Hitachi industrial area, located just 50 miles north of Tokyo. Everyone was quite excited at the prospect and there were some wild conjectures at the site which would be presented by the furiously burning plant buildings. Our group proceeded to the coast under the cover of darkness and probably arrived in position for the bombardment unobserved. If we did, we caught a lot of the Japs at work in the mills and other factory buildings and surprised them with about 1,500 tons of high explosives. After all the speculation as to what a rare sight or destruction would be, you can imagine the disappointment of all hands when they rushed up on deck after we finished only to discover that there was a terrific rainstorm raging and that you couldn't see beyond the end of your nose. The Alabama learned later that it had done a very handsome job of demolishing the targets assigned to her.

Despite the fact that Kenny was still serving onboard the *Alabama*, with the war's end and his service near its completion, he noted that everyone was already getting nostalgic for what they had experienced and accomplished.

Not too many of us share in her complete and brilliant record, but all of us have a very deep pride in having been part of her ship's company, for, to us, She has been the best ship in the US Pacific fleet and there is no man that will deny that her reputation is of the highest.

> This rather sounds like an obituary. In a way it is, for in every nook and corner, the men are sitting around in groups dreaming of home and counting up points scores. And everywhere there is the sad realization that the best crew that ever served together is about to break up it is the end of a grand association together and makes you feel sad in the same sort of way you felt when it came time to leave school and all the old comrades you knew and with whom you had shared countless experiences, both good and bad. When one of these groups grows silent, it is this nostalgic feeling that always makes someone say, "Do you remember—?"

Kenny Cooper ended his long chronicle with these words to Fred:

> Any day now will bring the formal end to the war and we hope to have an opportunity to get an eye full of Tokyo. But of course that is all another story and we'll have to wait for the time being. Who knows, perhaps before I can get the chance to write again about all of this, I may be telling you personally about it. But that is still a fond wish and something of which to dream.
>
> For now I shall just say so long,
>
> I remain your pal,
>
> Ken

When his service was done, Kenneth Cooper returned home to Saint Charles County. He married and had a long career at McDonnell Douglas as a draftsman. He passed away in 2010 and is buried in Saint Charles Memorial Gardens. His obituary noted that memorials could be made to the USS *Alabama* Memorial Fund. The "Mighty A" was forever in his thoughts.

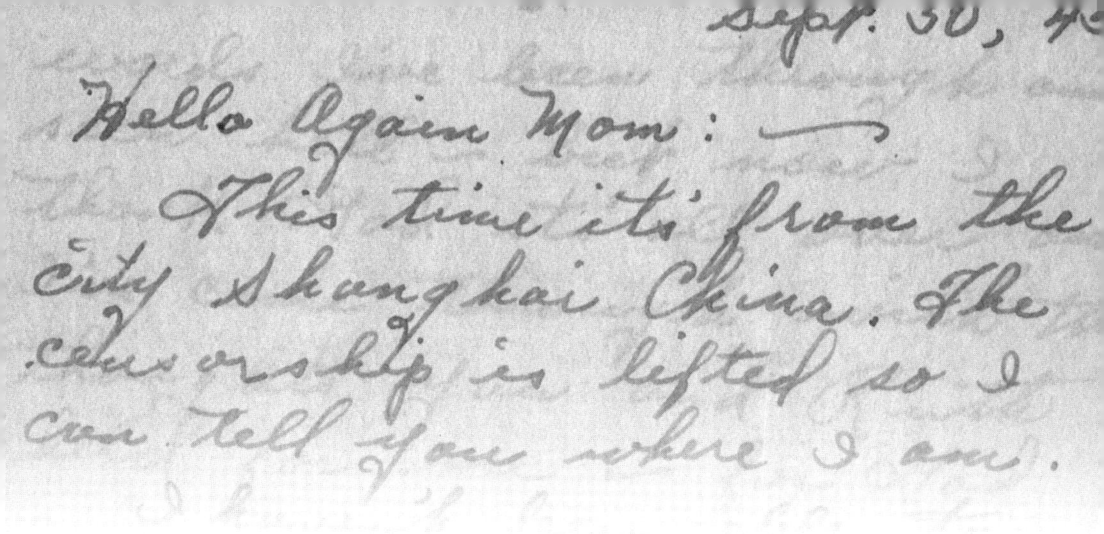
Sept. 30, 45

Hello Again Mom: —

This time it's from the city Shanghai China. The censorship is lifted so I can tell you where I am.

Joseph Mosar letter, September 30, 1945. *Collections of the Missouri Historical Society*

"IN PLAIN WORDS I'VE BEEN THROUGH AND SEEN HELL . . . NOW I THANK GOD IT'S ALL OVER."

— PETTY OFFICER JOSEPH A. MOSAR, US NAVY

This piece of correspondence seemed the most fitting for ending this compilation of letters. It encapsulates the words and feelings of most men who fought in both theaters of war during World War II. When V-J Day ended the formal hostilities in the Pacific, everyone breathed a sigh of relief and dreamed of going home. Joseph Mosar was no exception. He had only one goal, to get home to his wife, Ruth, and his mother, Florence, and resume life as it had been before the war.

Mosar grew up in St. Louis but left to take a job with Eastman Kodak in Rochester, New York. When the war began, he enlisted in the Navy. His photography skills were recognized, and he was sent to the Navy's Photographic Centers in Anacostia, Washington, DC, and then to Naval Air Station, Pensacola, Florida.

Sept 30, '45

Hello Again Mom:

This time it's from the city Shanghai China. The censorship is lifted so I can tell you where I am.

I haven't been able to write before this because I've been traveling day and night—Working the same but now it is all over and I'm here just awaiting transportation back to the States and home

I can't tell you of all the places I've been and things I've done in writing. It'll take months—to pack it in a few words or lines. I've been all over China—behind the Jap lines dressed as a coolie on the coast under fire—in plain words I've been through and seen hell—back now I thank God it's all over and I've come through with the thoughts you and Ruth held for me—for God only knows at times if it weren't for my constant thoughts of Ruth you and home I'll have gone stark mad.

My only concern now is for myself—in this respect since I've reached civilization again. I'm a pretty hardened person in speech and actions. I hope by the time I hit the states it will all have passed and I'll be my old normal self again.

Mom—just think I'll be home for Christmas this year, Xmas of '45. I have enough points and I've already been to the top from the Admiral, captain on down for my release and at last I've been put on the non essential list and as soon as possible, that transportation is available I'm on my way. The word so far is three to four weeks from this date. Now I'm praying to God that it's so.

With this word mom I'm going to say goodnight to you before I have to write to my Ruth before I can go to bed—so—it's bye bye for now and lots and lots of love and I'll be seeing you soon and we'll all be together this Xmas.

Bye for now

Son

Little is known of Mosar's service beyond what he mentions in his letter to his mother, which consisted of active combat behind Japanese lines in China. Whatever he experienced, it left him, in his own words, "a pretty hardened person."

We can hope that Mosar found some peace in the years after his return and that his desire to go back to his prewar state of mind was fulfilled. Happily, he got his wish to come home to Ruth. Soon after his return, they adopted a little girl. He passed away in 1998 and is buried in Rochester, New York.

But no man or woman who served returned home as the same person. Trauma cannot be forgotten, only recognized and brought to bear through treatment and reflection. Some came to terms with what they endured, but many did not. The men and women of World War II who were lucky enough to come home would never forget what it was like to suffer through the extreme heat of the North African desert, the jungles of New Guinea, or the Philippines, or the brutal cold of Alaska, the North Atlantic, or the forests of Belgium in winter. They could not unsee the extreme brutality of the Nazis toward the civilians of Europe or the cruelty of Japanese Imperial soldiers across the Pacific. And perhaps most horrible of all, they could never forget the pain of losing their friends, loved ones, or comrades to the violence of war.

Through courage and determination, they freed continents from the ignorance and brutality of two of history's most dangerous authoritarian regimes. But what many did went beyond the confines of the war. Women like Adela Riek Scharr and her fellow WASPs and African American pilot Christopher Newman and his comrades in the Tuskegee Airmen broke gender and race barriers for future generations and paved the way for integration of the military and expanded roles for women. If not for all their brave and selfless deeds, there is little doubt that the modern world would be a much darker place.

We will never truly understand what they went through. We can only be thankful and deeply appreciative of their service, dedication, and sacrifice. In the words of Sir Winston Churchill, "Never was so much owed by so many to so few."

Photo of Joseph Mosar. *Collections of the Missouri Historical Society*

The Court of Honor of World War II was dedicated on May 31, 1948. The ceremony at Soldiers Memorial included a parade of 10,000 marchers and an unveiling of the tablets inscribed with the names of those St. Louisans who gave their lives in World War II. The unveiling was led by Mrs. Ernest Roeher, a Gold Star Mother whose twin sons were lost in the war, and Lt. General Jonathan Wainwright, who was forced to surrender to the Japanese at Corregidor in the Philippines in 1942 and spent three years as a POW. *Collections of the Missouri Historical Society*

A FEW CLOSING WORDS

St. Louis too would not be the same after the war. Like most American cities, it witnessed a time of unprecedented growth and transformation. Federal programs like the GI Bill provided those who, prior to the war, could not afford a college education with access to universities like never before. Tens of thousands of St. Louisans saw their livelihoods improve by means of education and economic progress.

Easy access to home loans and a construction boom saw the rise of the St. Louis County suburbs and the expansion of development in St. Charles and other surrounding counties. Further economic changes brought by the war led to such things as strengthening the rise of St. Louis as a center of American aviation resulting in companies like McDonnell Douglas and later Boeing becoming major employers in the region.

But as populations shifted, it resulted in a complex mix of progress and decline that continues to this day. Eighty years after the war, the region still struggles with these complexities. It illustrates how impactful an event such as this can be a catalyst for change both good and bad. As time goes by, the changes World War II brought to St. Louis and the region will continue to both benefit and challenge us. We can build upon the good, but like those who faced the burdens of that conflict, it is up to us to find the right solutions to the problems that remain, no matter how daunting. We owe it to the memory of those men and women who gave their best when we needed them.

SOURCES

Archival Sources

National Archives and Records Administration

Missouri Historical Society

St. Charles County Historical Society

St. Louis County Parks and Recreation

St. Louis Public Library

School Sisters of Notre Dame Archives

State Historical Society of Missouri, The

Newspapers

Fulton (MO) *Daily Sun-Gazette*

Mexico (MO) *Weekly Ledger*

Popular Bluff (MO) *Daily American Republic*

St. Louis *Argus*

St. Louis *Globe-Democrat*

St. Louis *Naborhood Link News*

St. Louis *Post-Dispatch*

Washington (MO) *Citizen*

Webster Groves (MO) *News-Times*

Books

Baime, A. J. *The Accidental President: Harry S. Truman and the Four Months that Changed the World*. Mariner Books: New York, 2018.

Congdon, Don, ed. *Combat WWII European Theater of Operations*. Arbor House Publishing, 1983.

Congdon, Don, ed. *Combat WWII Pacific Theater of Operations*. Arbor House Publishing, 1983.

Ehlmann, Steve. *Crossroads: A History of St. Charles County, Missouri*. Lindenwood University Press, 2004.

Kraus, Theresa L. *China Offensive*. US Army campaigns of World War II. Center for Military History. Washington, DC: 1996, Gov Doc. CMH Pub 72-39.

Luebbers, George. *Hessoun Bohemian Catholic Orphanage 1908 through 1954*. Fenton Historical Society, Fenton, Missouri.

Morgan, Thomas D. "The Industrialization of World War II: America Goes to War." *Army History*. Spring 1994. No. 30 (Spring 1994), pp. 31-35.

Sherman, Steve. *The Life of James Sherman, 1911-1991*. Self-published, no date.

The War against Germany and Italy: Mediterranean and adjacent areas. United States Army in World War II. Pictorial record CMH pub volume 12-2. Washington, DC: Center of Military History, US Army.

Websites

Alabama III (BB 60), 1942-1962, history.navy.mil/research/histories/ship-histories/danfs/a/alabama-iii.html

American Air Museum, americanairmuseum.com/stories/no-mail-low-morale-importance-letters-wwii?utm_source=chatgpt.com

American Forces Network Online, media.myafn.dodmedia.osd.mil/FactSheets/2017_History_of_AFN_Fact_Sheet.pdf

Ancestry, ancestry.com

Cuba Route 66 Mural City, cubamomurals.com

Denshu Digital Repository, https://ddr.densho.org/media/ddr-densho-1007/ddr-densho-1007-6-1-transcript-29c099e476.htm

FindaGrave, findagrave.com

Fold3, fold3.com

International Churchill Society, winstonchurchill.org/resources/speeches/1940-the-finest-hour/their-finest-hour

Missouri Historical Society, mohistory.org

National Archives and Records Administration, nara.gov

National Park Service, nps.gov

National World War II Glider Pilots Association, ww2gp.org/CG-4A/stlouiscrash.php

National World War II Museum, nationalww2museum.org

Naval History and Heritage Command, history.navy.mil/research

OutLook by the Bay, outlookbythebay.com/of-local-interest/2014/06/when-the-war-came-to-the-bay

St. Charles County Executives Blog, sccmo.org/Blog.aspx?IID=187&ARC=444

State Historical Society of Missouri, The, shsmo.org

Teaching American History.org, teachingamericanhistory.org/document/bennett-champ-clarks-defense-of-the-first-neutrality-act

US government publications, govinfo.gov

Warfare History Network, warfarehistorynetwork.com/article/the-murmansk-run-running-the-gauntlet-of-wwiis-arctic-convoys

Women's Airforce Service Pilots (WASP) – Air Force Historical Support Division, afhistory.af.mil/FAQs/Fact-Sheets/Article/458964/womens-airforce-service-pilots-wasp

Youtube, Interview with Veteran Ralph Barrale, youtube.com/watch?v=nm8rBaI-jqY

INDEX